HOW SCHOOLS THRIVE

BUILDING A COACHING CULTURE FOR COLLABORATIVE TEAMS IN PLCs AT WORK®

foreword by **Robert Eaker**

THOMAS W. **MANY**
MICHAEL J. **MAFFONI**
SUSAN K. **SPARKS**
TESHA FERRIBY **THOMAS**

Solution Tree | Press

555 North Morton Street

Bloomington, IN 47404

800.733.6786 (toll free) / 812.336.7700

FAX: 812.336.7790

email: info@SolutionTree.com

SolutionTree.com

Printed in the United States of America

Library of Congress Cataloging-in-Publication Data

Names: Many, Thomas W., author.
Title: How schools thrive : building a coaching culture for collaborative teams in PLCs at work / Thomas W. Many, Michael J. Maffoni, Susan K. Sparks, Tesha Ferriby Thomas.
Description: Bloomington, IN : Solution Tree Press, 2019. | Includes bibliographical references and index.
Identifiers: LCCN 2019023394 (print) | LCCN 2019023395 (ebook) | ISBN 9781947604599 (paperback) | ISBN 9781947604605 (ebook)
Subjects: LCSH: Professional learning communities. | Teaching teams. | Mentoring in education. | Teachers--Professional relationships.
Classification: LCC LB1731 .M337 2019 (print) | LCC LB1731 (ebook) | DDC 371.14/8--dc23
LC record available at https://lccn.loc.gov/2019023394
LC ebook record available at https://lccn.loc.gov/2019023395

Solution Tree

Jeffrey C. Jones, CEO
Edmund M. Ackerman, President

Solution Tree Press

President and Publisher: Douglas M. Rife
Associate Publisher: Sarah Payne-Mills
Art Director: Rian Anderson
Managing Production Editor: Kendra Slayton
Senior Production Editor: Suzanne Kraszewski
Content Development Specialist: Amy Rubenstein
Proofreader: Kate St. Ives
Text and Cover Designer: Abigail Bowen
Editorial Assistant: Sarah Ludwig

All of us have had coaches who played an important role in our lives. To us, both personally and professionally, Rick and Becky DuFour were the consummate coaches. They were our biggest cheerleaders and supporters. They made us believe that we could accomplish anything and were making a difference in the world.

As leaders, authors, colleagues, and friends, Rick and Becky showed us how to lead by example. When faced with a challenge, they would roll up their sleeves and work side by side with us, articulating a clear vision of the desired future and identifying specific strategies that would lead to better outcomes.

Rick and Becky also showed us the importance of having a sense of urgency about this work. They didn't get caught up in the over-analysis of perceptions, data, or time-consuming planning processes. Instead, they led their schools and districts by learning together, translating research into practice, creating solutions to problems, and moving quickly to turn ideas into concrete action steps. They showed us that talking endlessly wouldn't solve anything; only people doing the work would.

We are forever grateful to have been coached, mentored, and influenced by Rick and Becky. They were masterful educators who embodied the essential elements of collective inquiry, continuous improvement, action orientation, and a focus on results each and every day.

—TOM MANY AND SUSAN SPARKS

"If you have seen further it is on the shoulders of giants."
—Sir Isaac Newton

To my "giants," Dr. Deena Tarleton and my late dear friend Dr. George Dietrich: Any career path that spans over thirty years and many changes requires mentors who are willing to walk beside you. Thank you for affording me the gift of seeing further as a teacher and a leader and allowing me to thrive. Your imprint on my career and my heart remain.

—MICHAEL MAFFONI

To Laura Jacobi, Carrie Korican, and Sunshine Weber, the best teacher team and group of friends a girl could ever ask for. Of course, I could not have written a single page without the love and support of my Tony and Elise. I love you both with all my heart.

—TESHA FERRIBY THOMAS

ACKNOWLEDGMENTS

A project like *How Schools Thrive* is a team effort. We would like to thank the whole team at Solution Tree Press; they are the best in the business! In particular, we want to recognize the incredible support we have received from Suzanne Kraszewski (our editor extraordinaire!) who is simply the best of the best! We sincerely thank you for the patience, effort, and expertise you showed in editing our manuscript. Finally, we appreciate the ongoing encouragement we received from Douglas Rife; we could not have done this without you!

Solution Tree Press would like to thank the following reviewers:

Jack Baldermann
Principal
Westmont High School
Westmont, Illinois

Taylor Barton
Principal
Lake Forest Elementary School
Sandy Springs, Georgia

Janna Cochrane
Principal
North Greenville Elementary School
Greenville, Wisconsin

Jamie Lakey
Assistant Principal
Coppell Middle School North
Coppell, Texas

Kathy Liston
Instructional Coach
Brookview Elementary School
West Des Moines, Iowa

Joshua McMahon
Principal
Morton West High School
Berwyn, Illinois

Debra Prenkert
Director of Elementary Education
Monroe County Community School Corporation
Bloomington, Indiana

Luke Spielman
Principal
Park View Middle School
Mukwonago, Wisconsin

Brenda Vatthauer
Principal
Lincoln Park Middle School
Duluth, Minnesota

Visit **go.SolutionTree.com/PLCbooks** to download the free reproducibles in this book.

TABLE OF CONTENTS

Reproducible pages are in italics.

CHAPTER 2

PART II

CHAPTER 3

CHAPTER 8

CHAPTER 9

APPENDIX A

APPENDIX B

APPENDIX C

ABOUT THE AUTHORS

Thomas W. Many is an educational consultant in Denver, Colorado. Tom retired as the superintendent of schools in Kildeer Countryside CCSD 96 in Buffalo Grove, Illinois. Tom's career included twenty years of experience as superintendent, in addition to serving as a classroom teacher, learning center director, curriculum supervisor, principal, and assistant superintendent. District 96 earned the reputation as a place where the faculty and administration worked together to become one of the premier elementary school districts in the United States during his tenure as superintendent.

Tom has worked with developing professional learning communities in school districts around the world. He has proven to be a valuable resource to those schools beginning their journey, offering special insights into developing the kind of coaching cultures that support the creation of high-performing collaborative teams.

In addition to more than fifty articles, Tom is the coauthor of *Amplify Your Impact: Coaching Collaborative Teams in PLCs at Work*®; *Learning by Doing: A Handbook for Professional Learning Communities at Work, Third Edition* with Richard DuFour, Rebecca DuFour, Robert Eaker, and Mike Mattos; coauthor of *Concise Answers to Frequently Asked Questions* with Mike Mattos, Richard DuFour, Rebecca DuFour, and Robert Eaker; a contributing author in *The Collaborative Teacher: Working Together as a Professional Learning Community*; coauthor of *Aligning School Districts as PLCs* with Mark Van Clay and Perry Soldwedel; and coauthor of *How to Cultivate Collaboration in a PLC* and *Leverage: Using PLCs to Promote Lasting Improvement in Schools* with Susan K. Sparks.

To learn more about Tom's work, follow @tmany96 on Twitter.

Michael J. Maffoni, an educator since 1987, has a diverse background that includes experience as a teacher, principal, and central administrator in a variety of districts in Colorado. He also teaches courses in educational leadership as an affiliate faculty member at Regis University.

Michael is the former director of professional learning communities (PLCs) for Jeffco Public Schools in Golden, Colorado. During his tenure, Michael led PLC implementation in over one hundred schools throughout the district. His collaborative leadership was instrumental in developing integrated PLC support systems, monitoring processes, and aligning professional learning. Three schools in Jeffco are nationally recognized model PLC schools.

Michael specializes in increasing educator and student learning by developing agency to coach and support collaborative teams. Additionally, he coaches leadership teams to scale PLC implementation in any size school system, both large and small.

He has presented at state and national events on topics related to continuous improvement for schools, teams, and individual educators. Michael has coauthored articles on increasing the effectiveness of collaborative teams and is a coauthor of *Amplify Your Impact: Coaching Collaborative Teams in PLCs at Work.*

To learn more about Michael's work, follow @mjmaffoni64 on Twitter

Susan K. Sparks is an educational consultant in Denver, Colorado. Susan retired in 2008 as the executive director of the Front Range BOCES (board of cooperative educational services) for Teacher Leadership, a partnership with the University of Colorado at Denver. Susan spent her career in St. Vrain Valley School District as a teacher and with four different BOCES as staff developer, assistant director, and executive director. She consults internationally in collaborative cultures, conflict resolution, contract negotiations, and community engagement.

She provides professional development and training in facilitating professional learning communities, impacting results through interpersonal effectiveness, managing challenging conversations, and creating collaborative teams.

Susan contributed to *The Collaborative Teacher: Working Together as a Professional Learning Community* and coauthored *Amplify Your Impact: Coaching Collaborative Teams in PLCs at Work* and *How to Cultivate Collaboration in a PLC* and *Leverage: Using PLCs to Promote Lasting Improvement in Schools.*

To learn more about Susan's work, follow @sparks12_susan on Twitter.

Tesha Ferriby Thomas is a school improvement facilitator and language arts consultant at the Macomb Intermediate School District in Macomb County, Michigan. She has worked in this capacity since 2012, supporting struggling districts and school leaders by helping them embed systemic practices that result in improved student achievement. Her passion for the power of PLCs has grown over twenty years as she has worked to support PLC implementation as a teacher, department chairperson, assistant principal, and assistant superintendent for curriculum and instruction. She is a coauthor of *Amplify Your Impact: Coaching Collaborative Teams in PLCs at Work*. She presents regularly at local, state, and national conferences on topics ranging from writing across the curriculum to implementing an instructional learning cycle in a PLC. She has been a member of the Michigan Learning Forward board and the Michigan Department of Education Surveys of Enacted Curriculum Steering Committee, and is a National Writing Project fellow. She is also a doctoral candidate at the University of Michigan Flint where she is researching the impact of coaching on PLCs.

To learn more about Tesha's work, follow @tferribythomas on Twitter.

To book Thomas W. Many, Michael J. Maffoni, Susan K. Sparks, or Tesha Ferriby Thomas for professional development, contact pd@SolutionTree.com.

FOREWORD

By Robert Eaker

It's no secret; the use of high-performing teams is a powerful way to improve organizational effectiveness—including schools! And the use of collaborative teams isn't new. As a young Marine recruit at Paris Island, South Carolina, in 1962, I distinctly recall an officer emphasizing that the entire United States Marine Corps was built on one overarching idea: a Marine rifle squad consisting of twelve Marines who work together (*interdependently*), to accomplish a shared mission (*common* goals), for which they hold each other accountable for success (*mutually accountable*). Think about that! The United States Marine Corps understood the power of collaborative teaming in 1962—in fact, long before that!

Since the mid-1950s, the use of high-performing collaborative teams has become so commonplace in organizations of all types, all over the world, that it is not even discussed anymore. There is an exception, however. Sadly, the norm for American education is still one of teacher isolation. In most schools, *individual* teachers are expected to ensure their students learn more standards than ever before, at higher levels of rigor, and in increasingly adverse conditions. This disconnect between what is known to be "best practice" (collaborative teaming) and what actually occurs (teacher isolation) is one of the great mysteries of modern educational practice.

However, there is good news! The increasing popularity of the Professional Learning Communities at Work® (PLC) framework has resulted in more schools embedding collaborative teaming into district and school structures and cultures. In short, in a high-performing PLC, collaborative teaming is not viewed as an innovation or initiative, or a unique structure to try. Instead, collaborative teams are seen as the engine that drives virtually every aspect of what occurs day in and day out. In PLCs, collaborative teams are the vehicle by which data-driven, research-based best practices are embedded within the daily routines of the district office, schools, teams, individual classrooms, and importantly, the support staff. In a highly effective PLC the use of collaborative teaming has become simply "How things are done around here!"

An important caveat is in order; in and of itself, collaborative teaming will do little, if anything, to improve student learning. Collaborative teaming is a vehicle—a *means* to an end, not an *end* in and of itself. Effectiveness—improved student learning—will be determined by the quality of the work being done by teams. Effective teams engage in the right work, in the right ways, at the right times, and for the right reasons!

Engaging teams in the right work will not happen by accident or invitation. If teams are to thrive, they need a number of things such as a rationale (the why for each task, product, or activity), time to meet, training, examples, monitoring, feedback, encouragement, support, along with frequent and timely celebration. In short, teams need to be effectively *coached*!

It's not enough to merely recognize that supporting and improving team effectiveness can be accomplished through coaching. The issue is what are concepts, practices, procedures, and tools that educators can use to effectively coach teams? What tools are available to coach coaches? How can coaches get better? In *How Schools Thrive*, Thomas W. Many, Michael J. Maffoni, Susan K. Sparks, and Tesha Ferriby Thomas present research-based concepts, practices, and protocols that can enhance team effectiveness and are grounded in years of successful practice. The result is a collection of tools that leaders can implement, in a reasonable amount of time, and when taken together and used with fidelity, are proven to be effective.

How can teams and coaches keep "getting better" in a culture that, by its very definition is never ending? The answer, in part, lies in continually *drilling deeper* into the work, coupled with sharpened specificity. *How Schools Thrive* moves far beyond how to effectively coach teams in addressing the three big ideas of a PLC (a focus on learning, collaborative teaming, and a focus on results.), or the four critical questions associated with learning (What is essential that all students learn? How will we know if each student is learning—skill by skill? How will we respond as a school and as a team when students struggle with their learning? And, how will we extend the learning of students who demonstrate proficiency?) The authors provide specific suggestions and protocols for drilling deeper into both the structural and cultural aspects of embedding the characteristics of a high-performing PLC into each team—task by task.

Drilling deeper implies, in part, making conscious what is often unconscious. For example, many teams simply evolve (or devolve) into a set routine that is rarely examined. In *How Schools Thrive*, Many, Maffoni, Sparks, and Thomas provide specific ideas for coaching teams into developing effective routines, tasks, and habits that revolve around such practices and collective inquiry, developing an action orientation that is reflected in action-research, creating a sharp focus on results—improved student learning—all within the framework of continuous improvement.

Of course, it is difficult—if not impossible—to coach a team into enhanced effectiveness unless teams recognize a sense of urgency. Readers of *How Schools Thrive* will find ideas for collaboratively analyzing data to create an accurate picture of a team's (or school's) current reality and pragmatic ideas, practices, and protocols for developing specific plans for moving forward, In short, *How Schools Thrive* is a resource designed to coach those who coach teams. The bottom line is this: just as improved student learning is inextricably linked to adult learning, adult learning is linked directly to the learning of those whose task it is to help teams improve. Helping teams thrive depends on coaches thriving. The ideas, concepts, practices, protocols, and other resources inside this book are powerful tools for enhancing team performance and ultimately student success. What is more important than that?

INTRODUCTION

Coaching-based initiatives are being leveraged and developed to support and change organizational cultures strategically and with positive results.

—HELEN GORMLEY & CHRISTIAN VAN NIEUWERBURGH

In our first book together, *Amplify Your Impact: Coaching Collaborative Teams in PLCs at Work* (2018), we introduce a framework for coaching collaborative teams in a Professional Learning Community (PLC) at Work. In that book, we share examples of how coaching improves a team's professional practice around the three big ideas—a focus on learning, a collaborative culture, and a results orientation—and the four critical questions—What do we want our students to know and be able to do?, How will we know when they learn it?, What will we do when they don't learn it?, and What will we do when they have learned it?—of a PLC (DuFour, DuFour, Eaker, Many, & Mattos, 2016). In this companion book, *How Schools Thrive: Building a Coaching Culture for Collaborative Teams in PLCs at Work*, we share more concrete ideas and strategies for coaching collaborative teams around the successful implementation of the essential elements of a PLC. We have created this resource to use either in tandem with *Amplify Your Impact* or separately on its own.

Both texts explicitly advocate for and identify the advantages of a shift from coaching individual teachers to coaching teams of teachers. Both books are grounded in the PLC process and both focus on promoting the development of highly effective collaborative teams. Both *Amplify Your Impact* and *How Schools Thrive* are anchored in the concepts of clarity, feedback, and support and promote the use of tools like the strategy implementation guide (SIG) and the Pathways for Coaching Collaborative Teams (pathways; Thomas, 2016) to assist those who coach collaborative teams.

Although the two books share many common elements, they are different in other ways. A useful construct for understanding the differences is based on the work of Ron Heifetz and Marty Linsky (2002). Heifetz and Linsky (2002) believe that change presents itself as a bundle of technical problems and adaptive challenges, but that change never involves exclusively one or the other—technical problems or adaptive challenges. Solutions to technical problems are fairly quick, straightforward, and readily apparent, while answers to adaptive challenges typically take longer, are more nuanced, and are less obvious. Clearly, PLCs have both technical problems and adaptive challenges.

In *Amplify Your Impact*, we offer specific strategies that help teams with the implementation of the more explicit tasks of PLCs—things like prioritizing and unwrapping standards, identifying learning targets, developing common assessments, holding productive data conversations, and using protocols to ensure that results—not best intentions—drive decisions. These tasks are the most common starting places for schools working to become a PLC and are more closely aligned with the kind of technical problems Heifetz and Linsky describe.

In *How Schools Thrive*, we shift our attention to coaching teams around the essential elements of the PLC process—continuous improvement, collective inquiry, action orientation, and a focus on results—and make a conscious effort to drill deeper into the more complex aspects of the PLC process. Mastering these PLC essential elements share many of the characteristics Heifetz and Linsky (2002) identify as adaptive challenges.

Taking PLC Practice to the Next Level

In an effort to improve their schools, principals often ask, "What's the next level of PLC training?" Or they might say, "My staff is ready for the next generation of PLC workshops." This kind of thinking reflects the notion that advanced training equals advanced content and levels of proficiency, similar to the way algebra II follows algebra 1, but the truth is there is no PLC Plus or PLC 2.0. The elements of the PLC process are constant, and while the big ideas and basic tenets don't change, what does change is the depth at which teams understand, and the fidelity with which they apply, the PLC process to their teams and in their schools.

During his work in schools, Richard DuFour, one of the architects of the PLC at Work® process along with Robert Eaker, often shared that principals frequently asked him about the availability of advanced levels of PLC training. Rick always answered their question same way: "There are no advanced levels of PLC training; we didn't hold anything back." He would continue this thought with, "We have shared our best thinking about how to ensure high levels of learning for all; you must now go back to school and do something with what you have learned." Bob Eaker agreed, adding that while there are no advanced levels of PLC *training*, he believed that teams can move beyond initial levels to more sophisticated levels of PLC *practice*.

We agree with both DuFour and Eaker; there are no advanced levels of PLC training, however, there are advanced levels of PLC practice. So, instead of asking about the next level of PLC workshops or training, a better question for principals would be, "How can we move teams to the next level of PLC practice?" For more and more principals, the answer to this question is found in the idea of coaching collaborative teams around improving their professional practice.

Eaker explains that teams in the early stages of the PLC process are focused on "getting started" and improve their practice when they begin to "drill deeper" (personal communication, 2018). When teams are getting started, they focus on putting structures in place. They work on things like developing a common language and establishing norms. They might prioritize and unwrap the standards to identify the highest leverage learning targets. Initial steps might also include designing common assessments, using protocols to facilitate productive data conversations, or creating master schedules that allow students to access more time and support without missing direct instruction in another subject. As terrific as all this work might be, Eaker suggests that improving a team's practice requires that teams drill deeper into the PLC process.

When teams drill deeper, they work on the same big ideas and basic tenets as other teams that are getting started, but as they drill deeper, these teams acquire new insights, confront new questions, and explore new approaches that may promote higher levels of student learning. For example, teams might shift from analyzing scores generated on traditional assessments to using student work to measure learning or move beyond identifying learning targets to developing learning progressions that describe what proficiency would look like for each of the priority standards. These teams are focusing on the same work as the teams that are getting started, but at a deeper and more sophisticated level.

Eaker believes that not all teams, just like not all students, will learn and make adjustments in the same way, whether they are just getting started or drilling deeper; some teams will grow further and faster than others. He explains that teams can drill deeper by (1) adding more specificity to their practice, (2) monitoring their progress, and (3) celebrating their improvement efforts (personal communication, 2018). Principals, assistant principals, curriculum supervisors, instructional coaches, department chairs—virtually anyone serving in a coaching role—can accomplish all three of these outcomes when they coach collaborative teams.

We see it all the time: coached teams are more effective than uncoached teams, and schools go farther faster when the primary goal of coaching is to help collaborative teams, rather than individual teachers, improve their professional practice. For example, the positive impact of coaching teams was apparent during a recent action research project conducted during the 2018–2019 school year at the elementary level in Macomb County, Michigan (Thomas, 2019). The researcher's purpose was to ascertain the impact coaching teams have on teachers' efforts to improve their instructional practice. The project was based on the assumption that the more teachers reflect on their instructional practices as a team, the more likely those practices will improve.

To determine whether coaching has any impact, the researcher observed multiple team meetings, some with a coach present and others without a coach present. The researcher collected data on the number of times teams engaged in self-reflection on their own practices—a hallmark of teams moving from getting started to drilling deeper—and the results were encouraging. When a coach was present in the observed team meetings, teachers reflected on their practice an average of 6.5 times, compared to only 1.6 times when no coach was present. By coaching teams through the PLC process, there is an increased likelihood that teachers will reflect on their practice, thereby increasing the likelihood of improved student achievement.

Eaker makes a persuasive argument in support of coaching collaborative teams (personal communication, 2018), but anecdotal evidence is also beginning to emerge that supports his belief that schools can and do continue to improve their PLC practice. The findings from this action research would suggest that the best way to advance a team's PLC practice and move them from getting started to drilling deeper is to consciously coach collaborative teams around the work of a PLC.

In *Amplify Your Impact* and again in *How Schools Thrive*, we propose that using a set of tools, the SIG and the pathways tool, helps support a coach's work with collaborative teams in a PLC. It is helpful to consider the tools an airline pilot uses to understand the purpose and differences between these two tools.

Using Tools to Drill Deeper

Most would agree that being a commercial airline pilot is a complex and sophisticated job that takes years of training and hours of practice to master all of the skills necessary to safely fly an airplane. Most would also agree that lives are on the line if a pilot does not execute his or her job responsibilities correctly. Like a pilot, a teacher works a complex and sophisticated job that takes years of training and hours of practice to master the skills required to ensure that all students learn at high levels. It is also true that for a teacher, lives are also on the line.

When a pilot prepares to fly a plane full of passengers to a destination, he or she is required to file a flight plan. The flight plan clarifies where the plane is going and ensures the pilot has thoughtfully planned the most efficient and effective route possible. As the pilot creates the plan, he or she must take into consideration a variety of factors such as distance, weather, and the amount of fuel required to reach the destination. An effective flight plan confirms that the pilot has carefully considered all options and alternatives to ensure the plane safely reaches its destination in the shortest amount of time.

In addition to filing a flight plan, the pilot must run through a preflight checklist to verify that all of the details required to fly the plane safely are in place. This detailed listing includes checking routine but necessary items such as flaps, lights, and electrical circuits, just to name a few. It is interesting that, even after years and years of repeated practice, all pilots must go through this list of particulars, in a prescribed order, checking and double-checking dozens of details.

Flight plans and a preflight checklist are designed for pilots flying commercial aircraft, but there are similar structures with many of the same characteristics available to educators engaged in the PLC process. The SIG and pathways tools have been instrumental in coaching collaborative teams toward improved effectiveness and, as a result, improved student achievement.

The SIG

The SIG we introduce in *Amplify Your Impact* supports the development of highly effective collaborative teams. The SIG guides teams and provides them with direction as they make progress toward their goal of improving their PLC practice. The most effective principals and coaches have found SIGs to be an excellent way for teams to identify their current reality, clarify their next steps, and build their capacity to execute various elements of the PLC process. Much like the pilot's flight plan, teams follow the SIG to help them move to the next level of best practice in the shortest amount of time possible.

In *Amplify Your Impact* we detail how schools can develop a SIG based on five prerequisites of a PLC (Many, Maffoni, Sparks, & Thomas, 2018).

1. Educators work in collaborative teams and take collective responsibility for student learning rather than working in isolation.
2. Collaborative teams implement a guaranteed and viable curriculum, unit by unit.
3. Collaborative teams monitor student learning through an ongoing assessment process that includes frequent, team-developed common formative assessments.
4. Educators use the results of common assessments to improve individual practice, build the team's capacity to achieve its goals, and intervene and enrich on behalf of students.
5. The school provides a systematic process for intervention and enrichment.

When collaboratively developed, a SIG promotes ownership of the PLC process and provides a roadmap for improvement. This tool can also be called a continuum or rubric. Some schools use rubrics for evaluative purposes while continuums represent resources that guide the curriculum's development. To be as precise as possible, we chose the term *strategy implementation guide* to describe the tool we use to help teams improve their PLC practices.

- *Strategy* acknowledges that PLC is our choice for an overarching school-improvement plan of action.
- *Implementation* describes the process coaches and teams engage in to create the conditions for high-performing collaborative teams.
- *Guide* conveys how coaches will use the document to provide feedback to teams.

The SIG allows coaches and teams to monitor their progress, determine current levels of collaborative practice, provide differentiated feedback, identify next steps, and set new goals.

The structure of the SIG unwraps the components of the PLC process by identifying anchor statements detailing the highest level of performance related to each of the five prerequisite conditions of a PLC. Additionally, each anchor statement is deconstructed into a series of descriptors placed along a continuum of implementation to identify the actions and behaviors of highly effective collaborative teams (see figure I.1).

Anchor Statements	Beyond Proficient	Proficient	Below Proficient
Educators work in collaborative teams, rather than in isolation, and take collective responsibility for student learning.	Teachers meet weekly in collaborative teams for a minimum of sixty minutes during the regular school day. They utilize norms, goals, and protocols and work interdependently to improve their practice and enhance student learning.	Teachers meet weekly in collaborative teams for a minimum of forty-five minutes during the regular school day. They write norms and goals, and participate in common planning to improve student learning.	Teachers meet weekly in collaborative teams for a minimum of forty-five minutes per week outside the regular school day. They work together on topics of mutual interest and share ideas, materials, and resources.
Collaborative teams implement a guaranteed and viable curriculum, unit by unit.	Teams prioritize and unwrap standards, identify learning targets, write *I can* statements, create common pacing guides, and commit to teach—rather than cover—the curriculum.	Teacher teams prioritize and unwrap standards, identify learning targets, and follow pacing guides created by the district or the publisher.	Teachers deliver lessons based on what they know the best, like the most, have materials for, or what is included in the textbooks.

Anchor Statements	Beyond Proficient	Proficient	Below Proficient
Collaborative teams monitor student learning through an ongoing assessment process that includes frequent, team-developed, common formative assessments.	Teacher teams work collaboratively to create valid and reliable common formative and summative assessments they administer every few weeks throughout the school year.	Teacher teams share the responsibility for creating common formative and summative assessments they administer on a regular basis throughout the school year.	Teacher teams rotate the responsibility for creating common summative assessments they administer periodically throughout the school year.
Educators use the results of common assessments to improve individual practice, build the team's capacity to achieve its goals, and intervene and enrich on behalf of students.	Teacher teams analyze common formative and summative assessment results to identify which students need more time and support and which instructional strategies they should retain, refine, or replace.	Teacher teams analyze the results of common formative and summative assessments to identify which students need more time and support.	Teacher teams review summative assessment results to monitor student progress or generate grades.
The school provides a systematic process for intervention and enrichment.	Teacher teams provide students with enrichment and remedial support as well as targeted and timely interventions that are systematic, practical, effective, essential, and directive, without missing direct instruction in another core subject.	Teacher teams provide students with remedial support as well as targeted interventions that are systematic, practical, effective, essential, and directive.	Teacher teams provide students with opportunities to receive additional remedial support.

Source: Many et al., 2018, pp. 59–60.

Figure I.1: Anchor statements in a SIG.

Visit ***go.SolutionTree.com/PLCbooks*** *for a free reproducible version of this figure.*

Teams begin the improvement process by reviewing the individual descriptors within a particular row of the SIG. In doing so, they identify which aspects of the PLC process are going well and which need more attention. Next, teams develop specific plans designed to move them from where they are to where they want to be. During this second step of the process, the SIG serves as a guide and helps teams monitor their progress. Finally, because SIGs represent an agreed-on standard of best practice, teams build on their own sense of efficacy as they make progress toward the goal of improving their PLC practice.

The process of creating a SIG requires schools to take into consideration varying factors that might alter their path and proactively identify alternative possibilities should any of those factors come to pass. Just like the pilot's flight plan, the SIG is designed to become a plan for moving collaborative teams to an agreed-on destination in the most effective and efficient way possible.

In this book, we highlight the role of a coach in using element-specific SIGs while working with teams to develop the essential PLC elements of collective inquiry, continuous improvement, action orientation, and a focus on results.

The Pathways for Coaching Collaborative Teams

A similar connection can be made between the pilot's preflight checklist and a team's pathway tool. The concept behind the pathways is to identify the most critical and important steps in the PLC process and ask probing questions that move teams through a series of tasks in response to the four critical questions of a PLC (DuFour et al., 2016). Each task a team tackles in response to the critical questions could be considered a part of the preflight checklist that ensures the routine but necessary elements of an effective PLC are in place and working properly. Figure I.2 shows the pathway tasks associated with each of the critical questions of a PLC. These tasks reflect the fundamentals of the PLC process.

A parallel exists between the pilot's preflight checklist and a team's pathway tool. The concept behind the Pathways is to identify the most critical and important steps in the PLC process and ask probing questions as teams move through a series of tasks in response to the four critical questions of a PLC. Each task in response to the critical questions could be considered a part of the preflight checklist that ensures the routine, but necessary elements of an effective PLC are in place and working properly.

As an example, the tasks associated with responding to question 1, What do we want our students to know and be able to do?, include prioritizing standards, identifying learning targets, determining proficiency levels, planning units, and analyzing strategies. Coaches can help teams use the pathways to monitor the presence and effectiveness of the various essential elements. If teams discover implementation gaps, coaches can provide extra time and support to ensure the various tasks are aligned to best PLC practice. Just as a plane cannot fly if its flaps are not working properly, collaborative teams will not maximize student learning if the basic tenets and big ideas of a PLC are not in place.

Critical Question One: What knowledge, skills, and dispositions should every student acquire as a result of this unit, this course, or this grade level?	**Critical Question Two:** How will we know when each student has acquired the essential knowledge and skills?	**Critical Question Three:** How will we respond when some students do not learn?	**Critical Question Four:** How will we extend the learning for students who are already proficient?
We're doing the following to answer this question:			
Prioritizing standards	Creating common formative assessments	Analyzing strategies (Teams will engage in similar practices at different stages of the instructional cycle, so there will be repeats.)	Planning enrichment activities
Identifying targets	Analyzing student work	Reviewing assessments	
Determining proficiency	Analyzing assessment data	Planning classroom interventions	
Planning units		Utilizing a system of support	
Analyzing strategies			

Figure I.2: Pathways as they relate to the four critical questions of a PLC.
Visit ***go.SolutionTree.com/PLCbooks*** *for a free reproducible version of this figure.*

Something to keep in mind about a flight plan and a preflight checklist is that it is important to have both; they work in tandem. A pilot could have a flight plan that provides a clear understanding of where he or she is going and how to get there, but if he or she fails to engage in the preflight checklist and something is wrong with the mechanics of the plane, the pilot may never get off the ground. Likewise, a pilot could implement the preflight checklist, but without a flight plan, he or she could end up flying in circles. The same is true for the SIG and the pathways in a PLC; both are necessary for the development of highly effective collaborative teams.

Applying the Best Thinking

With *How Schools Thrive*, we do not attempt to create a new theory or model; instead, we hope to apply the best thinking in our profession to the goal of creating highly effective collaborative teams. We cannot take credit for identifying the essential elements of a PLC; the recognition for that goes to Rick DuFour and Bob Eaker, as the architects of the PLC process.

We also want to acknowledge the seminal work of Peter Senge, the author of *The Fifth Discipline* (1990). In his writings, Senge urges leaders to create learning organizations. Educators can draw parallels between Senge's learning organization and PLCs. Senge (1990) argues that "what has been lacking is a discipline for translating individual vision into shared vision—not a 'cookbook' but a series of principles and guiding practices" (p. 9). We agree, and while many principles of Senge's learning organization are reflected in the PLC process, we believe there is also a need to translate the good things we know about coaching individuals around improving their instructional practice into a shared vision of coaching collaborative teams around improving their PLC practices.

Since the release of *Amplify Your Impact*, we often hear comments like, "OK, you convinced me; it's a good idea to coach collaborative teams, but can you tell us exactly *what* we should coach teams to do that will contribute to high levels of learning for all?" Good question! Once schools commit to coaching as the primary means of improving the effectiveness of PLCs, principals, coaches, and teacher leaders can more readily influence the way collaborative teams engage in the work.

This book will help identify the specific behaviors, routines, and habits that support a commitment to coaching collaborative teams. Creating a coaching culture while simultaneously promoting the team's mastery of collective inquiry, continuous improvement, action orientation, and a focus on results through the use concrete tools and strategies such as a strategy implementation guide and pathways tool is the focus of *How Schools Thrive*.

This book is divided into three parts. The first two chapters make up part I, "Making a Commitment to Coaching Teams."

Chapter 1, "Coaching to Create Habits of Professional Practice," explains *how* coaching helps collaborative teams identify specific tasks, create effective and efficient routines, and develop effective and efficient habits of professional practice.

Chapter 2, "Identifying How the Essential Elements of a PLC Thrive in a Coaching Culture," describes the impact that a healthy and resilient coaching culture has on collaborative teams in a PLC and explores *what* the essential elements of a PLC represent and provides a working definition for collective inquiry, continuous improvement, action orientation, and a focus on results.

In part II, "Understanding the Essential Elements of Highly Effective Teams in a PLC at Work," we focus on drilling deeper within four essential elements of a PLC: collective inquiry, continuous improvement, action orientation, and focus on results.

Chapter 3, "Learning Together—The Power of Collective Inquiry," defines collective inquiry and provides some pragmatic suggestions coaches should consider when promoting the idea that in a PLC, teachers begin the process by learning together.

Chapter 4, "Staying Restless—The Impact of Continuous Improvement," defines continuous improvement and presents a number of specific strategies coaches can employ to highlight the importance of using a systematic approach when helping teams improve.

Chapter 5, "Being Urgent—The Value of an Action Orientation," defines action orientation and offers several practical approaches coaches can use to help collaborative teams balance the right amounts of action and urgency.

Chapter 6, "Getting Better—The Significance of a Results Orientation," supplies coaches with a series of concrete steps to help teams understand that an authentic results orientation is more than test scores, dashboards, and scorecards.

The final chapters make up part III, "Coaching Collaborative Teams in PLCs at Work."

Chapter 7, "Assessing a Team's Current Reality," describes *how* those in coaching roles can assess the progress and development of collaborative teams with ways that coaches can use to differentiate clarity, feedback, and support based on the unique needs of individual teams.

Chapter 8, "Creating Collective Efficacy," describes the important impact of collective efficacy and explores how coaches can use the four sources of efficacy in their work with collaborative teams.

Chapter 9, "Creating an Action Plan for Coaching Collaborative Teams," presents a six-stage process school leaders can use to plan their coaching efforts.

The appendices present reproducible tools leaders can use to guide their coaching work with teams. Appendix A presents the stages of learning and essential elements of a highly effective PLC. Appendix B is an action planning template, and appendix C is a guide for communicating the action plan.

Moving Forward

Air travel has become a common experience for those visiting family, taking a vacation, or travelling for work; most of us have flown on a commercial airplane at one time or another. We enter the aircraft to a smiling crew member welcoming us aboard as we scan the row numbers and shuffle down the aisle. We squeeze into our seats, buckle up, and put our lives into the pilot's hands as we take off down the runway. Although most of us don't realize it, this experience is similar to what students go through every day. As we welcome them into the classroom with a smile and encouraging word, students also put their lives into our hands as we usher them onto a runway toward learning. It is our responsibility as educators to ensure that they arrive safely.

We believe if those in coaching roles will encourage mastery of the essential elements of a PLC, the result will be the development of highly effective collaborative teams in their schools. In *How Schools Thrive,* we provide concrete and specific ways that teams can dig deeper into their practice and foster advanced levels of PLC practice.

PART I

MAKING A COMMITMENT TO COACHING TEAMS

CHAPTER 1

Creating Habits of Professional Practice

The question is not do our teams have habits; the question is, "Do our teams' habits of professional practice promote high levels of learning for all?"

—THOMAS W. MANY

If the goal is to improve teaching and learning in our schools, and if the PLC process is the strategy school and district leaders choose to reach that goal, then leaders must help teacher teams improve their PLC practices. Highly effective collaborative teams have been called the foundation, the fundamental building block, and the engine that drives a PLC (Eaker & Dillard, 2017). Bob Eaker and Heather Dillard (2017) suggest that, "Just as it is generally recognized that districts must work to close learning gaps between subgroups of students, it is also district leaders' responsibility to close the effectiveness gap between collaborative teams within each school" (p. 47). Collaboration is not a new idea in schools; The PLC process—"an ongoing process in which educators work collaboratively in recurring cycles of collective inquiry and action research to achieve better results for the students they serve" (DuFour et al., 2016, p. 10)—creates learning environments in which learning is constant, and innovation and experimentation flourish.

Likewise, research has established that coaching is the most effective way to deliver job-embedded professional development to teachers. Matthew Kraft, David Blazer, and Dylan Hogan (2017) believe coaching is a "key lever for improving teachers' classroom instruction and for translating knowledge into classroom practices" (p. 7). The combination of coaching and collaboration represents our best opportunity to improve schools.

To ensure that collaborative teams within PLCs are functioning at the highest level, we contend that schools should commit to coaching collaborative teams. It may sound simple, but, to paraphrase Senge (1990), a school's commitment to, and capacity for, coaching can be no greater than that of its members. So, before deciding coaching is the way to go, principals, coaches, and teacher leaders should pause, reflect, and determine if they are truly ready to make such a significant commitment.

- **Commitment is a big deal.** It means going all in, no excuses or half-hearted efforts. Being committed means that you are willing to do whatever it takes. It means taking personal responsibility, and it requires looking in the mirror.
- **Commitment is long term.** It is pushing through the occasional ups and downs that are part of any improvement effort and choosing to create a vision for the future. It necessitates a persistent and ongoing effort to achieve a goal.
- **Commitment is emotional.** It is about engaging in the work with your head and heart; it compels us to care about each other both personally and professionally. Nothing meaningful is ever accomplished without embracing both the emotional and intellectual dimensions of the work.
- **Commitment is relentless.** It requires acting with a sense of urgency, and it demands an unshakable dedication to the success of an idea; it requires a willingness to reject other initiatives and continue "working on the work" until you get results.
- **Commitment is purposeful.** It means devoting sufficient resources and making necessary changes, even if they are hard. It requires aligning all of your policies, practices, procedures, and planning efforts to the singular goal of ensuring high levels of learning for all.

Those who commit to coaching collaborative teams create the conditions that expand the capacity of coaches to help teams get better at getting better. In these schools, the most effective principals and teacher leaders understand that coaching is not about having all the answers or simply telling people how to improve their practice; they also understand that coaching is not reserved for the select few who have the word *coach* in their job description or job title.

Leaders who commit to coaching embrace it as the primary way to deliver professional development to teachers. They are confident that, given the right opportunity, everyone will benefit from having the opportunity to be a coach and the most effective leaders will strive to create a school culture where everyone is willing to coach and be coached in an effort to improve their practice.

Schools committed to coaching believe that coaching should not be limited to new or struggling teachers but that everyone, even the most effective teams and individual teachers, can continue to learn and improve. In these schools there is a belief that everyone has something important to share with others, and thus, everyone is encouraged, even expected, to engage with colleagues to improve.

Five beliefs are present in schools where teacher leaders, coaches, and principals have committed to coaching as the vehicle for developing high-performing collaborative teams.

1. **Belief in the power of learning together through a process of collaboration and collective exploration:** In schools committed to coaching, everyone is willing to coach and be coached in the name of improving their collective practice.
2. **Belief that together we create better solutions than any of us do by ourselves:** Said another way, the smartest person in the room *is* the room. No one person has all the answers, but by working through a process of collective inquiry together, we create better solutions to new challenges than we can by thinking and working alone.
3. **Belief in other people and their potential to continuously learn and grow:** There is always room for improvement; in fact, it is the biggest room in the school. We can only improve our collective performance through continuous learning and improvement with a real focus on helping both individuals and teams realize their collective potential.
4. **Belief that challenges are opportunities for new learning, and that problems are best addressed through careful study and reflection:** If you're too busy to reflect, you're too busy to improve. We get the most out of people, not by telling, explaining, or even demonstrating what to do, but through engaging people in a process of action research and problem solving that helps them think through choices and options.
5. **Belief that we do the work we do to help us achieve the results we seek:** The best reason to engage in the intentional coaching of collaborative teams is to help teams get better at getting better, and, ultimately, achieve the results of higher levels of learning for all.

These beliefs are closely linked to the essential elements of a PLC as outlined in the definition of PLC: "an ongoing process in which educators work collaboratively in recurring cycles of collective inquiry and action research to achieve better results for the students they serve" (DuFour et al., 2016, p. 10). They serve as the foundation of coaching collaborative teams. In a PLC, teams must develop a certain degree of mastery over essential elements of the PLC process, which include collective inquiry, continuous improvement, action orientation, and a focus on results (which are the topics of the chapters in part II of this book). In schools committed to coaching, collaborative teams incorporate these elements—as well as the specific tasks, routines, and habits that support them—into their professional practice every day. PLC leaders must recognize that in order to ensure high levels of learning for all, it is not enough for teams in their schools merely to survive; teams must thrive.

Take a moment to think about how teams in your school develop habits of practice. Are their habits the result of a conscious, purposeful, and intentional process grounded in what research tells us about best practice, or have they evolved haphazardly in a random and arbitrary fashion over an extended period of time? And, to what are their habits of practice aligned? Have teams identified the mission-critical habits of practice they aspire to see in their school? Do the team's habits reflect the values, beliefs, and commitments of the school, or are they based on history, past precedent, and personal preference?

When teams have established the right habits for the right reasons, they can overcome any obstacle in their path. It matters not if they are challenged by a new set of standards, implementation of new curricula, or changes in student demographics; they will consistently respond in ways that promote high levels of learning for all.

Productivity and Collaborative Teams

It is the combination of effectiveness and efficiency that creates higher levels of productivity on collaborative teams. Teams become more effective when individual tasks are combined in routines and more efficient when the routines become habits of professional practice. The goal of those in coaching roles is to make the work of collaborative teams as productive as possible, and teams become more productive when they create positive habits around their professional practice. Coaches recognize that productive habits don't happen by chance; they develop as coaches and leaders support teams with ongoing clarity, feedback, and support.

As an example of the symbiotic relationship between effectiveness and efficiency, consider the activities or tasks associated with PLC critical question one, What do we want students to know and be able to do? (DuFour et al., 2016). Responding to question one requires teams to accomplish a number of individual tasks including prioritizing and unwrapping the standards, identifying high-leverage learning targets, developing learning progressions, and drafting student-friendly "I can" statements. Each of these individual tasks is beneficial in and of itself, but when a number of tasks or activities are combined into a single routine, teams amplify the impact of their efforts; said another way, the whole is greater than the sum of its parts.

As these routines become ingrained in the everyday working environment, they become habits of practice. Teams that develop habits of practice complete their work faster, with greater confidence, and more ownership of the outcome. In this case, when the way teams respond to question one becomes a habit, they no longer think about the individual steps associated with the task; they just do the work!

Oftentimes, teams new to the PLC process are given time to meet in collaborative teams without direction on how they should spend their time. Without guidance from someone in a coaching role, these teams may end up discussing topics like tardy policies, field trips, or discipline issues, which have nothing to do with responding to the four PLC critical questions or ensuring that all students learn to high levels. Unfortunately, when teams do not receive the kind of support and guidance that coaching can provide, the result is the development of unproductive habits that do not move teacher teams or student achievement forward. Therefore, it is imperative that leaders provide teams with differentiated coaching that helps them identify the tasks and routines that they must develop in order to create new habits consistent with the premises of the PLC process.

It is not uncommon for teams to develop inefficient and ineffective habits that are harmful to teaching and learning. These bad habits often develop precisely because teams have little or no coaching. Teams may be doing the best they can with what they know at the time, but simply lack the knowledge and leadership needed to move forward in a productive way. One of the key responsibilities of those in coaching roles is to help teams become more productive.

The Causes of Unproductive Habits

Teams become unproductive when members are unwilling or unable to do what must be done to ensure all students learn to high levels. Figuring out what is causing a team's lack of productivity is one of the hardest tasks school leaders must tackle. Principals, coaches, and teacher leaders often feel they are left with a binary choice: either the problem is a lack of will or a lack of skill. We think there is another possibility. Maybe the problem isn't a lack of will or skill; maybe the problem is a lack of coaching.

Some teams are not willing to commit to the views and values necessary for all their students to learn to high levels. For them, the *why* is not clear and their beliefs are not yet aligned with those of the PLC process. When a team is not committed to the idea that all students can learn, when teachers are struggling with their belief about student learning or their own ability to influence student success, when a team is having problems with the cultural elements of the PLC process, it manifests itself as a lack of will. Coaches respond to a lack of will by guiding the team through a series of reflective conversations that help teachers examine the impact their current values and beliefs are having on student learning.

Other teams may not have enough experience or a deep enough understanding of what must be done to ensure high levels of learning. These teams just don't know how to do the right work and have yet to develop the habits necessary to successfully implement the PLC process. When teams are not confident they can do the work and teachers are struggling with the structural elements of the PLC process—identifying learning targets, creating common assessments, using data to drive instruction, or creating opportunities for students to receive additional time and support—it manifests itself as a lack of skill. Coaches respond to the lack of skill by creating a specific set of learning opportunities designed to promote mastery of the activities and tasks necessary to be successful.

When the team does not have a sense of efficacy and the team is wrestling with both commitment and confidence, it manifests as resistance. Coaches can respond to resistance by supporting the team's efforts to set attainable goals and celebrate short-term wins.

What is clear is that whether the team's lack of productivity is due to the lack of will, skill, or some combination of both, those in coaching roles are in the best position to diagnose, differentiate, and deliver the clarity, feedback, and support teams need to increase their productivity by developing the right habits of professional practice.

How Habits of Professional Practice Are Formed

Without realizing it, we all practice a number of habits throughout the course of each and every day. For example, think about your morning wake-up routine. If you're like us, your alarm rings and you immediately press the snooze button (sometimes more than once), but you eventually swing your feet onto the floor and walk to the bathroom. You brush your teeth, take a shower, and dress for the day before heading to the kitchen for your coffee. You have developed each of these habits over time. They have become second nature. You don't have to think about them; they are a normal part of your everyday life. However, these habits were not always in place.

At some point in your life, you developed each of these habits individually. You learned that you would be late for school if you didn't set an alarm, so you started setting your alarm each night before bed. You learned the benefits of good hygiene, so you began taking daily showers and brushing your teeth. You also learned that caffeine helps provide the extra energy you needed to get your brain moving, so you bought a coffee machine to brew your morning java. One by one, you integrated each of these individual habits into your morning routine. You engaged in *habit stacking* (Clear, 2015; Kruse, 2017).

Similar to the development of morning habits, teams begin developing habits by engaging in small, individual tasks that provide opportunities for quick, short-term successes. Teams then turn these tasks into routines that members repeat over and over until eventually, the routines become habit. Those in coaching positions play an important role in monitoring the work and redirecting teams back to their routines when the team begins to veer off course. The graphic in figure 1.1 illustrates how habit stacking works.

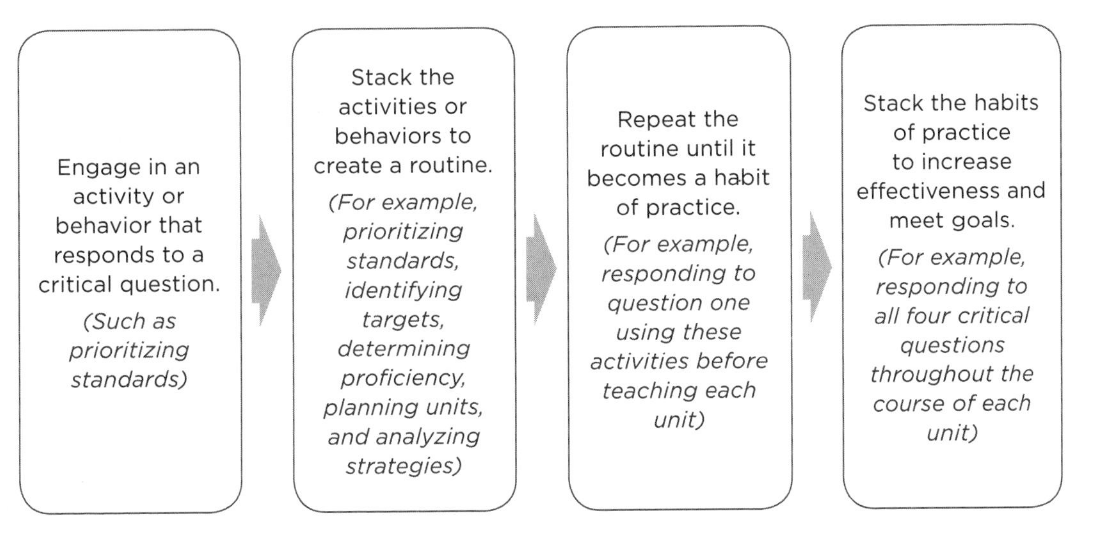

Figure 1.1: The process of habit stacking.

Anyone who has attempted PLC transformation knows it can be an overwhelming process requiring a large number of cultural and structural changes. However, implementing the PLC process is far more manageable when we break it down into bite-sized chunks instead of trying to eat the entire PLC elephant in one big bite. As coaches of collaborative teams in a PLC, we can help teams engage in habit stacking as a means of improving their PLC practice.

Individual tasks are the foundation of routine, and routines are at the heart of every habit. Habits form when people incorporate specific tasks into routines that they repeat regularly over an extended period of time. In a PLC, principals and coaches help collaborative teams identify the individual tasks that turn into routines that eventually develop into habits of professional practice.

The Role of Clarity, Feedback, and Support

Best practice can be habit forming if the right professional practices are present within a culture of collaboration; but without the right amount of clarity, feedback, and support, teams may never know which kind of habits they are developing—productive or unproductive.

Clarity: Creating Routines Around the Right Work

To bring greater clarity to the PLC process, principals and coaches should ask, "Are our collaborative teams clear about which practices deserve more time and attention?" If the mission is to ensure that all students learn at high levels, the first step in the process is to clarify which practices are critical to accomplishing that mission. Those mission-critical best practices are the tasks teams identify that turn into routines and eventually become habits.

Team meetings are filled with routines. Simply convening the weekly team meeting is a routine that becomes so commonplace teachers notice when they miss a meeting. Within the meeting there are other routines like reviewing the norms, stating the meeting's purpose, using an agenda, assigning roles and responsibilities, and relying on a consensus decision-making process. All of these routines help promote more productive team meetings.

More importantly, teams establish routines in response to the four critical questions of learning. They routinely begin the unit planning process by identifying and unwrapping the highest priority standards, drafting a common assessment, analyzing data and evidence of learning, and creating opportunities for students to access more time and support when they do or do not learn.

It is the role of the coach to help teams become clear and stay clear on what a team's "right work" truly is. The most effective teams have a clear understanding of the work they are being asked to do and engage in habits that help them accomplish their goals.

Feedback: Reinforcing Routines Around the Right Work

The right kind of differentiated feedback can ensure that a team's individual tasks, routines, and habits align with what we know is best practice. Effective feedback can do wonders when coaching collaborative teams around their routines and habits. Intentional feedback can reduce the risk teachers feel when trying new classroom strategies, it can encourage teachers to engage in deep self-reflection, and it can challenge team members to step out of their comfort zones. If coaches and principals focus on reinforcing the right work with the right feedback at the right time, the likelihood that teams will replicate that behavior increases.

Feedback from those in coaching roles can also confront behaviors that are counterproductive to the habits teams are trying to create and redirect routines when teams fail to engage in the right work. The goal should be to provide feedback that reinforces behaviors aligned with best practice, create routines that are repeated over an extended period of time, and encourage the development of productive habits of professional practice.

Support: Building Capacity Around the Right Work

The most effective principals and coaches view their role as one of building the capacity of teams to do the right work. Coaches should never do for teams what teams can do themselves, but coaches can help teams identify what practices are most important, create routines that support those practices, and guide the development of habits around each team's professional practice.

The support teams receive is invaluable; however, when a principal or coach sets the team's goals, analyzes their assessment data, or determines their next steps, they are not building the team's capacity. In fact, when those who coach start *doing* the work instead of *supporting* the work, they actually diminish the team's capacity.

Coaches should also be careful not to impose their own personal or preferred routines on teams. People support that which they help create, and so coaching is much more effective when the coaching focuses on helping teams identify the specific tasks that lead to the creation of routines and ultimately become habits of professional practice.

The Best Habits for Stacking: The Fundamentals

As in any athletic, artistic, or commercial endeavor, the PLC process can be broken down into a set of fundamentals that can be taught and improved upon with practice. Fundamentals are the basic, simplest, most important elements, ideas, or principles of what we are trying to accomplish. While it might seem like an oversimplification of the work we do to improve schools, it's true: *fundamentals are fundamental.* If you find you or your staff struggling with some aspect of the PLC process, go back to the fundamentals.

The good news is that educators have identified the fundamentals. There has never been a clearer consensus or greater agreement on what schools must do to positively impact student learning. The importance of a guaranteed and viable curriculum, common formative assessments, and systems of intervention are not up for debate. Neither is the idea that teachers should work together interdependently on collaborative teams. These are the fundamentals of high-achieving schools. Whatever teams are trying to accomplish, they must master the fundamentals to succeed.

In the early stages of becoming a PLC, many teachers can name the fundamental elements of the PLC process. They know there are three big ideas, and they can recite the four critical questions. But from time to time, they will confuse or conflate the meaning or application of each element with other initiatives. As teams progress in implementation, teachers begin to identify the individual tasks associated with each of the fundamental elements, recognize what must be done, and describe how the work is accomplished. When teacher teams fully transition into a PLC, they incorporate the fundamentals into their daily routines and apply them when working with new students, new materials, and new situations. For these teams, the fundamentals become habits of professional practice.

As an example of this progression, consider a focus on learning (the first of the big ideas). A focus on learning consists of four critical questions that teachers must respond to on a regular basis: What do we want students to know and be able to do? How do we know they have learned it? What do we do if they do not learn what is expected? What do we do if they do learn what is expected? In the early stages, most teachers can recite the four questions and may even be able to define the meaning of each, but principals should not assume that because teachers "know" these fundamentals of the PLC process they can do what it takes to be successful. This condition (consciously not doing what aligns with best practice) is what Jeffery Pfeffer and Robert Sutton (2000) describe as the *knowing-doing gap*.

Articulating the four critical questions is a good start, but it's not enough. Teams begin to close the knowing-doing gap when they respond to the four questions and identify a specific set of individual tasks associated with each question. For example, when responding to question one—What do we want students to know and be able to do?—teams must first identify the most essential standards, then unwrap the standards to determine which targets are the most important, and finally, turn their attention to developing the necessary success criteria, learning progressions, and I-can statements.

A comparable set of individual tasks is associated with question two—How do we know when they have learned it? When responding to question two, teacher teams identify the learning targets that students absolutely must know and be able to do, determine the level of rigor or cognitive demand for each target they will assess, select the most appropriate type of question or task to measure that target, and finally, create a test plan to ensure the validity and reliability of the assessment. The way teams respond to questions three and four—What do we do when students have or have not learned?—can be broken into a similar set of tasks.

When the fundamentals become a regular and routine part of a teacher's practice, they become habits of professional practice. So why is it that some schools are more successful than others when it comes to implementing the PLC process? It's all about turning the fundamentals of the process in habits of professional practice. Consider the following scenario.

Principal Stackhouse has decided to coach his language arts team toward improving the PLC process by devoting team time to creating routines and habits in response to the four critical questions of a PLC, beginning with question one, What do we want students to know and be able to do as a result of this class, course, or grade level?

Principal Stackhouse begins by utilizing the Pathways for Coaching Collaborative Teams, which helps his team identify and engage in the following tasks related to question one.

- Prioritizing and unwrapping standards
- Identifying learning targets
- Determining proficiency levels
- Drafting I-can statements
- Planning units and assessments
- Analyzing strategies

The language arts team intentionally practices the first pathways task, prioritizing and unwrapping the standards, before team members start teaching their next unit. It is difficult at first, but they follow the pathway and come to consensus on the priority standards for the unit. The team moves on to prioritize and unwrap the standards for the next unit, and then the next. After practicing with multiple units, the task of prioritizing and unwrapping standards develops into a routine. The team continues using the routine it built around standards with the units for the remainder of the year, which eventually turns the routine into a habit.

As the team continues to practice the habit of prioritizing standards, members shift their focus to the task of determining the highest leverage learning targets. With the help of the coach, the team creates another routine to identify learning targets and practices it until this new routine also becomes a habit. The principal and his coach help the team stack the second habit of identifying learning targets on top of the first habit of prioritizing and unwrapping standards. In so doing, they build the team's capacity to function more productively as part of a PLC.

Moving Forward

The goal of coaching collaborative teams is to help teams get better at getting better, and in a PLC, the most effective teams develop habits of professional practice around the right work. Principals and coaches help clarify which mission-critical practices teams should embrace, provide teams with the right kind of feedback at the right time, and support teams in their efforts to ensure all students learn to high levels.

Becoming a highly successful PLC can be daunting work that requires a significant amount of change for many educators, but principals and coaches can lessen the pressure and cognitive dissonance collaborative teams feel by explaining the impact of developing productive routines and habits of professional practice. Effective coaches help teams develop productive habits of practice by doing three things: (1) providing clarity on which productive routines to practice, and giving teams permission to focus on one or two routines at a time; (2) offering effective, actionable feedback as the team develops the routine into a productive habit; and (3) supporting teams through the process of stacking individual habits into even larger habits of professional practice.

Experts like Larry Boyle argue that coaching should focus on the team level (Forbes Coaches Council, 2016). According to Boyle, the key to developing a strong coaching culture is to "educate teams about what coaching is and then have them do it—coach each other" (p. 3). In the next chapter, we delve into the connection between coaching cultures, collaborative teams, and the essential elements of a PLC.

Summary

- The combination of coaching and collaboration represents our best opportunity to improve schools.
- Commitment means devoting sufficient resources and making necessary changes, even when they are difficult. It means aligning all policies, practices, procedures, and planning efforts to the singular goal of ensuring high levels of learning for all.
- *How Schools Thrive* offers an opportunity to highlight the role of a coach in developing the essential elements of collective inquiry, continuous improvement, action orientation, and a focus on results.
- Those who commit to coaching collaborative teams create the conditions for teams to get better at getting better.
- When teams have established the right habits for the right reasons, members will consistently respond in ways that promote high levels of learning for all.

- Teams become more effective when individual tasks are combined in routines and more efficient when the routines become habits of professional practice.
- Coaches can help teams identify what practices are most important, create routines that support practices, and guide the development of habits.
- Habit stacking is putting it all together and creating the most productive routines and habits of practice.
- Coaches should not do for teams what teams can do for themselves.

Reflection Questions

A coach plays an instrumental role in supporting teams in developing habits of professional practice that deepen their understanding of the PLC process. As you reflect on the content of this chapter, consider the following six questions.

1. What is your district, school, or team's commitment to coaching?
2. What does coaching currently look like in your system?
3. What conditions are needed to promote the implementation of coaching collaborative teams as a primary improvement strategy?
4. Describe your team's practices and habits. Are they grounded in research and aligned to the tenets of the PLC process? What would you change about your practices?
5. How would your team respond to the question, What are the fundamentals of the PLC process? Are there certain tasks and routines (related to the fundamentals) your team excels in or needs to work on?
6. What does habit stacking look like on your team? Can you describe any examples of habit stacking related to the four critical questions of learning?

CHAPTER 2

Identifying How PLC Elements Thrive in a Coaching Culture

Professional Learning Communities have emerged as arguably the best, most agreed-upon means to improve instruction and student performance.

—MIKE SCHMOKER

AllThingsPLC (2016) identifies the essential elements present in high-performing collaborative teams when it defines the PLC process as "an ongoing process in which educators work collaboratively in recurring cycles of collective inquiry and action research to achieve better results for the students they serve" (p. 6). This definition explains that educators work collaboratively, which is another way of saying that teachers learn together, and, while working in teams, participate in a process of *collective inquiry* to improve their practice. Next, this definition describes how teachers tackle the task of improving their practice as teams engage in regular cycles of *continuous improvement* and *action research*. Finally, it articulates the reasons why teams should engage in these actions: to achieve better *results* for the students they serve. By deconstructing the definition of PLCs, we can readily identify the essential elements of a PLC.

We believe the creation of a coaching culture by school leaders through the coaching of collaborative teams is wholly consistent and compatible with the process of becoming a PLC. In this chapter, we explore the relationship between the kind of culture that coaching should create with collaborative teams and the four essential elements of a PLC—collective inquiry, continuous improvement, action orientation, and a results focus— in order to elevate the performance of teams to a higher level of PLC practice.

The Impact of Coaching

Interest in the impact coaching cultures have on schools is growing (van Nieuwerburgh & Passmore, 2012); however, while the term *coaching culture* has become a part of the lexicon of American education, there is no agreed-on definition of what a coaching culture is or how it fits within the framework of the PLC process. This lack of clarity around a precise definition of a coaching culture or the relationship between coaching cultures and collaborative cultures has left principals, coaches, and teacher leaders with a host of questions about coaching cultures and the essential elements of a PLC, such as those we share in the following sections.

What Is the Relationship Between Coaching and Collaboration?

Jenkins (2018) makes it clear that a coaching culture is part of the larger context of an organization's collaborative culture, and, while the terms *coaching culture* and *collaborative culture* may share some of the same characteristics, a coaching culture is best thought of as a subset or extension of a school's collaborative culture. As Leadership that Works (2019) notes, "The research is clear . . . coaching improves performance, collaboration, and output" (p. 1).

What Does the Research Say About the Value of a Coaching Culture?

Research has established the positive impact coaching cultures have on organizations (International Coaching Federation [ICF], 2014). One of the findings of the ICF (2014) study is that, in addition to improved employee performance, organizations with strong coaching cultures tend to have much higher levels of employee engagement. Higher levels of engagement generate positive effects such as the following three.

1. Increased levels of ownership (employees take more responsibility for achieving organizational goals)
2. Healthier and more productive responses to new challenges (employee responses to change are more resilient)
3. More creativity and agility (solutions to problems are more innovative)

In a 2017 ICF study, 80 percent of the respondents who received coaching support reported benefits such as improved performance, better communication skills, enhanced productivity, and growth in their sense of well-being.

In 2018, the ICF reported that high-performing organizations (schools) with coaching cultures in place "have stronger change management capabilities" (p. 3) and argue that "coaching is one of the most helpful ways to develop these capabilities" (p. 4).

Importantly, the results of the ICF survey confirm that organizations with "strong coaching cultures are also more likely to have better talent and outcomes, and success at large-scale strategic change" (p. 4).

Our experience coaching teams has shown us that teachers in schools with strong and resilient coaching (and collaborative) cultures respond to challenges differently than teachers in more traditional school cultures. Given what researchers have found, imagine how teachers working in a school with a healthy coaching culture might respond to the introduction of a new set of standards. Instead of waiting to comply with an external mandate, teacher teams would commit to working together to understand how the new standards might impact their teaching (collective inquiry). The team's efforts would result in a plan (action orientation) for effectively and efficiently incorporating the new standards into their instructional practice (continuous improvement) that would ultimately lead to higher levels of student achievement (results orientation).

The ICF (2018) finds that among organizations *with* a strong coaching culture, 61 percent are also classified as high-performing organizations. However, among organizations *without* a strong coaching culture, only 27 percent are classified as high-performing organizations. In other words, "Strong coaching cultures are more that twice as likely to be high-performing organizations" (ICF, 2018, p. 19).

What Constitutes a Strong Coaching Culture, and How Do I Recognize One When I See It?

The ICF (2014; 2017) uses a set of six criteria to determine if an organization has a strong coaching culture. If we translate their criteria developed for the private sector into the parlance of education, we would find the following to be true in schools with strong coaching cultures.

1. Teachers value coaching.
2. Administrators value coaching.
3. Coaching is available to every member of the faculty and staff.
4. Money and other resources are specifically allocated to support coaching.
5. Internal coaches, external coaches, and administrators spend time interacting with others in coaching relationships.
6. A wide range of individuals deliver coaching support.

The first two criteria are self-explanatory; coaching is a valued part of the school's culture. In schools with healthy coaching and collaborative cultures, coaching is seen as the primary vehicle for delivering professional development. Not only do educators in these schools value coaching, but the most effective leaders understand that coaching is beneficial for individual teachers *and* collaborative teams!

In addition, a strong coaching culture does not limit coaching to beginning teachers or those on performance-improvement plans. Leaders take conscious and intentional steps to ensure that coaching is easily accessible and widely available to everyone, whether effective or ineffective, experienced or beginning, master or novice.

Equally important, schools with strong coaching cultures find ways to commit resources such as time, money, and personnel to support coaching. Evidence of this commitment can be seen in the way leaders organize the master schedule, allocate and utilize staff, and provide ongoing training opportunities for members of the faculty and staff.

Similarly, there is sufficient capacity available from internal and external coaches, teacher leaders such as department chairs and grade-level leads, and administrators—even the teacher teams themselves—to provide coaching opportunities when needed. Leaders plan and execute coaching support in ways that ensure teachers get timely feedback.

Finally, the word *coach* is no longer seen as someone's title, specific position, or designated role. In schools with strong coaching cultures, individuals who fulfill different roles and come to the coaching relationship with different backgrounds and experiences deliver the coaching. These schools acknowledge that depending on the situation, everyone can coach and be coached. In these schools, a coaching culture exists "when a coaching approach is a key aspect of how the leaders, managers, and staff engage and develop all their people" (Hawkins, 2012, p. 21).

What Are Some Characteristics of a Strong Coaching Culture?

As is the case with collaborative cultures in a PLC, coaching cultures are both structural and cultural. If one's perspective is structural, coaching would be viewed as a set of skills and strategies that are used to enhance teachers' effectiveness. Gill Buchanan (n.d.) explains:

> The desired outcome [of a coaching culture] is a collaborative approach to creating a culture in which every member of the organization recognizes the benefits of coaching, understands how to respond to coaching techniques, and actively demonstrates coaching skills and behaviors themselves.

Nancie J. Evans (2011) says school leaders with a structural point of view would likely focus on "evidence of coaching in the day-to-day interactions throughout the organization" and look for evidence of employees "listening, asking questions, and probing in a manner that encourages understanding, reflection, learning, and change" (p. 37). From a structural perspective, Evans (2011) would encourage school leaders to look for opportunities to leverage the skills and strategies of coaching to improve a team's PLC practice.

If the assessment is that coaching is more cultural in nature, principals, coaches, and teacher leaders would likely see coaching as a set of beliefs that drive an organization's behaviors. Similar to the notion that a PLC is not something you do, a PLC is something you are, Diana Anderson and Merrill Anderson (2005) believe that "coaching is more than a set of skills; it is a rich, holistic approach for releasing the potential in people and organizations." (p. 127).

When school leaders subscribe to a cultural perspective, Evans (2011) believes the faculty and staff would "genuinely believe that coaching is the way that they need to interact and work together to achieve the organization's goals and fulfill its purpose" (p. 38). She argues that the challenge for principals, coaches, and teacher leaders "is not to create a coaching culture, but to identify the ways that coaching interacts with, and acts upon, other elements of an organization's culture to achieve its goals and fulfill its purpose" (p. 46).

According to Gill Buchanan (n.d.), "A coaching culture will look different in every organization as it will be developed to compliment the overall culture of the [organization]." Evans (2011) agrees and suggests that "most organizations are better served by focusing on the value that coaching can provide as part of a culture that is aligned with its strategy and goals than by creating a coaching culture" (p. 45). She recommends that leaders do the following:

> Create a coaching culture where coaching is embedded in the way that people work in a day-to-day basis. In other words, leaders should work to create a culture where coaching occurs formally and informally between people at all levels within and across functions and departments. (p. 36)

Buchanan (n.d.) and Evans (2011) both contend that if the overall culture of a school is collaborative, and if coaching is aligned with an organization's values and beliefs about the importance of collaboration, then the presence of a coaching culture will serve to further enrich the existing culture within the school.

Regardless of whether your perspective is structural, cultural, or some combination of both, what is clear is that the act of coaching and the creation of a coaching culture is process, not person dependent.

Can Coaching Change School Culture, and How Does It Impact Collaborative Culture?

We believe the answer is *yes*, coaching can change a school's culture! In schools where the students are learning, so too are the adults. Coaching cultures provide the ideal environment to nurture high levels of learning for all.

David Clutterbuck and David Megginson (2005) suggest that schools that create coaching cultures are "demonstrating a commitment to grow the organization alongside a parallel commitment to grow the people inside the organization" (p. 19). Carrie Lupoli (2018) agrees, noting that "coaching creates the conditions of excellence by increasing collaboration, individualizing support and improving teacher effectiveness faster than traditional professional development (PD) techniques" (p. 2).

Evans (2011) argues that it just makes sense: "If coaching changes people, and people create organizations by their social interaction, then coaching should change organizations" (p. 47). Helen Gormley and Christian van Nieuwerburgh (2014) agree, noting, "As coaching is said to support change in individuals and teams, it is fair to assume that coaching cultures will have organizational implications" (p. 93).

Since a successful coaching experience requires collaboration between a coach and an individual or team of teachers, we argue that a school cannot have a coaching culture without the kinds of relationships commonly found in an effective PLC. In fact, the results of a 2018 study by the ICF found that coaching-related activities were most helpful to leaders in achieving the desired changes.

Growing appreciation for coaching collaborative teams as a way to change the culture of an entire school supports the shift from traditional coaching models focused primarily on coaching individual teachers to more contemporary approaches orientated toward the coaching of collaborative teams. The takeaway for PLC leaders is that the conscious, purposeful, and intentional coaching of collaborative teams can change the culture of their school.

Who Can Coach, and Who Is Responsible for Creating and Maintaining a Coaching Culture?

Michael Moody (2017) believes that an effective coaching culture requires an entire ecosystem of support. He argues that what matters in a coaching culture is not who the coach is, but rather the quality of "the interactions between teachers and those around them" (p. 2). For Moody, providing the kind of high-quality feedback teachers need to continue improving their practice is only possible when a school's coaching efforts "are well-designed, well-coordinated, and involve multiple support providers, which may include administrators, instructional coaches, or colleagues" (p. 2). Moody's point is that a coaching culture is about coaching, not coaches.

Gormly and van Nieuwerburgh (2014) also believe there is plenty of evidence that coaching is a powerful way to help all teachers improve their practice, yet many schools limit the scope of coaching to a few beginning teachers or teachers on improvement plans. Elena Aguilar (cited in Greene, 2018) says that approach is a mistake and maintains that all teachers "deserve to keep growing" (p 4).

We have learned through our work in schools across the United States that a coaching culture is not the responsibility of a single individual. Experience has shown us that there are many people in schools who can coach, and while Moody (2017) acknowledges that instructional coaches are important members of a school's coaching ecosystem, he observes that "a coach is still just one person, and they don't solve everything" (p. 2).

An instructional coach might be considered the lead coach, but in most school districts, finding the resources to employ the number of coaches that would be needed to support all the teachers who would benefit from coaching is unrealistic; the way traditional instructional coaching roles are currently configured in most schools simply doesn't provide enough capacity. It is unlikely that schools will ever have enough coaches to support *all* the needs of *all* the teachers *all* the time; the impact of a school's coaching efforts, however, can be doubled, tripled, even quadrupled if the focus of a school's coaching efforts shifts from individual teachers to collaborative teams.

When creating a coaching culture, one of the biggest untapped resources principals, coaches, and teacher leaders have at their disposal are the teachers themselves. Moody (2017) maintains that "fellow teachers can act as effective coaches, even in an informal setting" and notes that "peer feedback among teachers can be a financially efficient (and time-efficient) way for principals to create opportunities for frequent instructional feedback" (p. 2). Moody (2017) identifies an additional benefit to teachers coaching teachers: "Through coaching, these teachers not only help to improve the practice of their colleagues, but also improve their own teaching practice. Good teachers have an avenue for professional growth by serving as coaches, thus feeding their need and desire to get better" (p. 2).

We have long believed that the primary purpose of coaching collaborative teams is to help teams get better at getting better. A team's efforts to ensure all students learn to high levels may have been led by any number of individuals including an instructional coach, department chair, principal or assistant principal, or the team may have embraced the opportunity to coach themselves and tackled the task with the confidence born of past success.

The key insight for school leaders is that in a healthy coaching culture, many different people must engage in the coaching of teacher teams around the cornerstone concepts of clarity, feedback, and support if we hope to provide teachers with what they need to succeed (Many et al., 2018).

In a PLC, collaborative teams commit to improve their practice by engaging in a process of *collective inquiry* through reoccurring cycles of *continuous improvement* coupled with an *action orientation* that is *focused on results*. Teams thrive when coaching cultures focus on these four essential elements of a PLC; in fact, we believe that creating a coaching culture is one of the most effective ways school leaders can promote the development of the essential elements. The final step is to identify and define the essential elements of a PLC.

Learning Together: Collective Inquiry

There is tremendous power in the communal exploration of professional practice. AllThingsPLC (2016) states that "Members of professional learning communities *always* attempt to answer critical questions by first learning together. They engage in collective inquiry to build shared knowledge" (p. 1). We see powerful examples of learning together in many aspects of the PLC process. Every time teachers participate in a team meeting, they have the opportunity to improve their practice. The simple act of identifying the highest priority standards and agreeing on the most essential learning targets deepens teachers' knowledge about what they want their students to know and be able to do. By working together to design, administer, and analyze common assessments, they sharpen their pedagogy as they share ideas on how to teach the same content or concepts differently. There is no doubt that the powerful effects of job-embedded professional development are best observed when teachers learn together and build shared knowledge through the process of collective inquiry.

AllThingsPLC (2016) explains why the process of collective inquiry is so important:

> This collective study of the same information increases the likelihood that members will arrive at the same conclusion. Members of a PLC, by definition, will *learn* together. . . . They [teachers] also build shared knowledge regarding the reality of the current practices and conditions in their schools or districts. (pp. 1–2)

By modeling a process of collective inquiry and consciously choosing to coach collaborative teams (as opposed to individuals), we acknowledge that no one person has all the answers and that by working together, teams will consistently generate better solutions than any individual teacher could by him- or herself. Learning together (collective inquiry) is an essential element of highly effective teams.

Staying Restless: Continuous Improvement

AllThingsPLC (2016) defines continuous improvement as "an ongoing cycle of planning, doing, checking, and acting designed to improve results—constantly" (p. 2).

When teams are constantly striving to improve their results, they are in what we call a "relentless state of restlessness" about their instructional practice.

Being restless means never being quite satisfied with the way things are; these teams understand that, as good as the team may be at any particular point in time, there is always room for improvement. Coaching teams to be restless about their professional practice is the best way to prevent teams from getting complacent with the existing state of affairs.

Teams that are restless about their practice have accepted continuous improvement as a regular and routine part of their work. They are comfortable asking questions such as, Is there a better way? or Can we achieve better results using some other approach? For these teams, asking questions is not seen as a reflection on the team's efforts thus far. Rather, questions are a manifestation of the belief that the regular and routine reflection on a teacher's professional practice promotes exploration, inquiry, and improvement. Embracing a relentless state of restlessness (continuous improvement) is the second essential element of a PLC.

Being Urgent: Action Orientation

In a PLC, there is a belief that challenges are opportunities for new learning, and that problems are best addressed through the careful study of, and reflection on, professional practice. Teams in a PLC believe that we get the most out of people, not by telling, explaining, or even demonstrating what to do, but by engaging them in a process of action research and problem solving that helps them think through choices and options.

Schools with an action orientation recognize that knowing is not enough; teams must act. According to Mike Schmoker (1999), the best schools "are concerned with processes only insofar as these processes affect results" (p. 5). While it is true that teams working in schools with an action orientation engage in specific strategies like action research and lesson study to identify the best alternatives, they also move quickly with a sense of urgency to apply their new insights in the classroom.

A common trait of teacher teams that demonstrate a sense of urgency is that they are learners themselves, constantly in search of a better way, but unlike their colleagues, they reject a shotgun approach to a laundry list of goals in favor of a laser-like focus on a limited number of goals. This disposition fosters the development of teams that are patient but determined to improve their practice; teachers on these teams view the school's current reality as nothing more than a great place to start the next round of improvement. In other words, they move from learning to doing with a palpable sense of urgency. A sense of urgency (action orientation) is the third essential element of a PLC.

Getting Better at Getting Better: A Results Orientation

A results orientation encompasses far more than test scores, and the results we seek are much more than numbers, ranks, and ratings. In most schools, far too much time is spent collecting, compiling, organizing, and admiring data, and far too little time is spent doing something, *anything*, with the data. Schmoker (1999) supports this when he says, "Results should take us beyond the exclusive use of such annual indicators as test scores and dropout rates" (p. 77). He continues, "Such data do not inform or derive from a teacher's ongoing and monthly efforts" (p. 77). It is time to stop pretending that the act of analyzing scores from national, state, and local assessments is enough to constitute an authentic results orientation. An authentic results orientation does not manifest itself solely in test scores, score cards, and dashboards.

The kind of results we seek in PLCs are changes in teachers' practice. Schmoker (2006) believes that, "When leadership is focused on *results*, on urging a formal, frequent review of the impact of instruction, teaching improves" (p. 126). John Hattie (2009) repeatedly encourages teachers to know their impact, and Judith Warren Little (1990) describes collaboration as the "thoughtful, explicit examination of practices and their consequences" (as cited in Schmoker, 1999, p.16). There is a consistent message here: instructional practice improves when teams of teachers focus on things like results, impact, and consequences. Helping teams get better at getting better (results orientation) is the fourth essential element of a PLC.

Moving Forward

The essential elements of collective inquiry, continuous improvement, action orientation, and results orientation are timeless, and, when teams incorporate them into their daily routines, they develop the habits of highly effective teams. Furthermore, we believe these essential elements are attainable by any faculty committed to the idea that the fundamental purpose of their school is to ensure high levels of learning for all.

Summary

- In a healthy coaching culture, everyone is willing to coach and be coached in an effort to improve; coaching cultures are about *coaching*, not *coaches*.
- Coaching cultures that primarily focus on coaching collaborative teams rather than coaching individual teachers can serve the needs of more teachers.

- School leaders can promote the development of the essential elements of a PLC by creating a coaching culture in their schools.
- Teams first learn together and engage in collective inquiry to build shared knowledge.
- Continuous improvement is an ongoing and continuous cycle that includes planning, doing, checking, and acting on results.
- An action orientation is when teams know that engaging in specific strategies like action research and lesson study propels a team to uncover what is working and what is not in their practice. Action-oriented teams move with a sense of urgency to apply new insights in teaching and learning.
- Teams have a results orientation when, instead of focusing on standardized test scores and dropout rates, teams focus on results, impacts, and consequences in their instructional practice.

Reflection Questions

A coach plays an instrumental role in supporting teams in developing advanced understanding and implementation of the four essential elements of a PLC outlined in this chapter. As you reflect on the content of this chapter, consider the following six questions.

1. How does your team embrace a relentless state of restlessness?
2. What behaviors and conditions need to be in place for your team to excel in collective inquiry?
3. What behaviors and conditions need to be in place for your team to excel in continuous improvement?
4. What behaviors and conditions need to be in place for your team to excel in having an action orientation?
5. What behaviors and conditions need to be in place for your team to excel in a results orientation?
6. Using the criteria of a strong coaching culture as your guide, what beliefs, behaviors, and conditions need to be in place for your school to develop a healthy coaching culture?

PART II

UNDERSTANDING THE ESSENTIAL ELEMENTS OF HIGHLY EFFECTIVE TEAMS IN A PLC AT WORK

CHAPTER 3

Learning Together—The Power of Collective Inquiry

We learn more by looking for the answer to a question and not finding it than we do from learning the answer itself.

—LLOYD ALEXANDER

Schools and districts that implement the PLC process at high levels channel resources to create a focus on learning. These schools place learning for all at the very center of their mission and understand that PLCs are a catalyst for student achievement. That spark ignites when teachers engage in collective inquiry.

In this chapter, we explore more deeply the meaning of collective inquiry in a PLC. We then examine the seven norms of collaboration and propose strategies for coaching the routines and habits of collective inquiry.

Understanding Collective Inquiry

Collective inquiry in a PLC is "the process of building shared knowledge by clarifying the questions a group will explore together" (AllThingsPLC, 2016, p. 2). In a variety of professions, inquiry is not only a centerpiece of best practice, but rather, a standard; it is the way to investigate multiple theories or hypotheses to generate deeper understanding and create new solutions or outcomes.

In the medical profession, collective inquiry is commonplace. Following a diagnosis of diabetes, a team is assembled to ensure optimal patient care. At the table are a primary doctor, endocrinologist, dietitian, nurse, ophthalmologist, podiatrist, and trainer. Each member of the team brings unique expertise and skills to the conversation. As the team dialogues, the members ask questions that deepen the knowledge of the collective group, and the conversation that ensues becomes a dynamic, ever-evolving process as members share more information.

The medical team considers past practices, both successful and not, the role the individual will play in treatment options, how family and caregivers support the individual, and his or her overall health status. Time is spent talking, thinking, and planning together to construct a common understanding. Most importantly, the team recognizes that each member holds an important perspective that benefits the patient's long-term health. To achieve this realization, the medical team must embrace that collective inquiry is not a linear process. Instead, it requires problem solving, full engagement, and a flexible mindset.

Like in the medical profession, collective inquiry is vital in a PLC; it serves as an essential element of the PLC process. Learning together and building shared knowledge by clarifying the questions that a group will explore together are the hallmarks of collective inquiry. Teams that intentionally practice effective routines associated with inquiry develop lasting problem-solving habits in their daily collaborative practice. These shifts toward collective inquiry develop a team's capacity to identify valuable new instructional methods to overcome complexities of learning for students in their school. When teams commit to learn and develop shared knowledge together, collective inquiry thrives. Figure 3.1 highlights benefits of a shift to collective learning.

Learning as Individuals	**Learning as a Team**
Examine needs and gaps in instruction based on one perspective.	Affords multiple perspectives as teams problem solve to identify needs and gaps in instructional practice.
Focus on independent practice where success is based on one individual's criteria.	Focus on interdependence and group success where all members are mutually accountable to common outcomes.
Teacher bias toward student learning could be present and remain unchecked based on limited individual teacher data.	Teacher bias toward student learning is checked based on availability of multiple data points and levels of results.
Instructional practices are limited by one's own background, schema, knowledge, and skill set.	Instructional practices are influenced by the sum of the group's backgrounds, schemas, knowledge, and skill sets
Professional learning happens through individual actions, professional reading, and 1:1 coaching	Job-embedded professional learning occurs through group dialogue and the team coaching model.

Figure 3.1: The shift to collective learning.

There are powerful benefits to building shared knowledge. Collective inquiry puts the onus of learning and results for *all* students and teachers in the hands of educators, not the default of a lockstep curriculum, pacing guide, or similar resource.

The essential element of collective inquiry is the byproduct of the types of questions teams investigate in a PLC. Among these are:

- What is it our students must learn?
- What is the best way to sequence this learning?
- What are the most effective strategies to use in teaching this essential content?
- How will we know when students have learned this content?
- How will we respond when students don't learn?
- What will we do when students already know this content?
- What can we learn from each other to enhance our effectiveness?

Each of these inquiry questions tightly align to the big ideas of a PLC and the four critical questions of learning (DuFour et al., 2016). When collaborative teams cycle through the PLC questions, they embrace collective inquiry as a habit of professional practice.

We, the authors, make the assumption that teams who embrace collective inquiry have the *will*—the passion, drive, curiosity, and commitment—to increase learning outcomes for all students. This is the mantra and mindset that we find in PLCs across the United States. What we notice is that despite the *will* for the work to happen, the *skill* often needs the support of a coach in order for collective inquiry to become a habit that promotes ongoing learning. Habits that establish the conditions for collective inquiry include attention to effective team structures and processes, intentional shifts in language, and use of open-ended questions.

Coaching Collective Inquiry Routines and Habits

Collective inquiry, the root of collaborative practice in a PLC, is centered on a process that includes the following components: identifying common barriers to student learning, setting goals, probing, questioning, and learning what practices work best to accomplish the goal.

Teams that learn and make meaning together outperform those that do not. Many structures exist to ensure this occurs. Collaborative teams look at common data and results to build awareness and set goals to improve instructional practices. They add to their toolkit by digging into research that supports their intended outcomes. Conducting observations and walkthroughs in other schools and classrooms can broaden perspective and add to instructional pedagogy. Actualizing similar technical approaches promotes alternative viewpoints. While technical approaches to learning and building shared knowledge are required for teams to be successful, and cannot be underestimated, the remainder of this chapter investigates how coaches can develop routines and habits that foster meaningful inquiry and interaction among team members within the structures of a PLC.

In order to maximize the engagement of teams in the collective inquiry process, coaches commit to developing the conditions for inquiry to flourish. If we are a PLC, then how we interact brings the PLC to life.

Highly effective collaborative teams hold meaningful conversations centered on the four critical questions of learning: (1) What do we want our students to learn?, (2) How will we know if each student has learned it?, (3) How will we respond when some students do not learn it?, and (4) How can we extend the learning for students who have demonstrated proficiency? (DuFour et al., 2016). These questions encourage teams to engage in the process of collective inquiry around teaching and learning.

The seven norms of collaboration (Garmston & Wellman, 2016) serve as a scaffold to enhance the level of a team's collaboration and decision making. They are as follows.

1. Promoting a spirit of inquiry
2. Pausing
3. Paraphrasing
4. Probing for specificity
5. Putting ideas on the table
6. Paying attention to self and others
7. Presuming positive intentions

Teams improve their use of the seven norms when the norms are embedded into the PLC process and supported by coaching. The following sections illustrate how the seven norms of collaboration align with a team's PLC practice.

Promoting a Spirit of Inquiry

Collaborative teams promote a spirit of inquiry when they value learning together and the ideals of curiosity, questioning, and continuous learning. When teams champion the inclusion of everyone's ideas, risk taking improves, enhancing outcomes. Teams that exhibit a spirit of inquiry will say, "We are working for all students," "We will face challenges and successes," "We don't know all the answers," and "We are in this together."

Pausing

During team meetings, the most proficient teams intentionally create time for their members to reflect. One or two individuals can dominate a team meeting; pausing slows the pace of conversation to assure that everyone is being heard and has time to reflect before responding. When a teammate pauses his or her thinking, collective inquiry thrives as the pause allows other ideas to surface. Members of teams that practice pausing might notice three to five seconds of silence before others respond to comments that a teammate has shared.

Paraphrasing

In the PLC process, teams actualize their full potential when they learn together and build shared knowledge. Paraphrasing is an excellent strategy to ensure that all individuals have the opportunity to clarify their thinking before moving on to the next speaker. Teams that develop paraphrasing as a habit of their professional practice reach higher levels of clarity. On a team where the norm of paraphrasing is present, you might hear teammates echoing the thoughts of their colleagues in search of clarification. These teams often use phrases such as, "So what you're saying is . . ." or "If I understood you correctly, you believe . . ." to preempt their paraphrasing.

Probing for Specificity

Highly effective teams probe for specificity by using open-ended questions that invite a speaker to fully explain his or her idea. Using the norm of probing for specificity assures each idea is clear and helps teams avoid acting on generalizations. When teams routinely practice probing for specificity, you hear, "Can you give us some more information on ______?" and "Help me understand what you mean by ______."

Putting Ideas on the Table

The collective intelligence of a team improves when members feel safe to share their thinking and put new or innovative ideas on the table. For collective inquiry to thrive, team members are encouraged, even expected, to share their ideas. Putting ideas on the table maximizes the opportunity for the team to learn from one another. Teams that practice putting ideas on the table say things like, "Let's make sure we hear from everyone," or "______, will you share your perspective on that idea?"

Paying Attention to Self and Others

Paying attention to self and others requires teams to become "people watchers" and pay attention to others' body language, voice intonation, and actions. When an individual is paying attention, you might notice body language like leaning in to hear a colleague speak. Most adults have never been taught skills related to nonverbal communication, but when done well, this norm helps build trust and empathy among team members. On a team that pays attention to self and others you might hear, "______, we haven't heard from you in a while. What are your thoughts on ______?"

Presuming Positive Intentions

Presuming positive intentions is a natural byproduct of teams whose individual members share a common conviction that all students can learn. Teams continually revisit the idea that the fundamental purpose of their school is learning, not teaching, and work to foster the belief that everyone is dedicated to ensuring that all students succeed. On a team that presumes positive intentions you hear statements such as, "I appreciate everyone sharing ideas" or "I believe we have similar goals for our students, and I was thinking . . ."

Using the Seven Norms of Collaboration in a PLC

Following are two examples that illustrate how teams use the seven norms of collaboration to strengthen collective inquiry. As you read, you will notice that neither example shows all seven norms being utilized in a single team meeting. The seven norms are not intended to be a checklist teams complete, nor is there an expectation that every one of the norms will be present in every meeting. As these scenarios show, coaches play an important role in helping teams to become more conscious and intentional about using the seven norms of collaboration to promote the development of collective inquiry as a habit of professional practice.

Example One: Secondary Language Arts Team

A secondary language arts team comprised of four teachers with varying levels of experience (two veteran teachers, one teacher in her fifth year, and a first-year teacher) meet weekly for planning. At this particular meeting, the team agrees to prioritize the standards related to an upcoming unit on the influence of setting on character development.

Within the first few minutes of the meeting, the veteran teacher pulls out the prior year's planning template and suggests that the team replicate the lessons since, according to her, the unit was highly successful. The new teacher listens and, respecting the opinion of the veteran teacher, agrees to teach the lessons as they had been taught in the past. However, the coach notices that the other two teachers quickly glanced at one another, but did not comment.

The coach decides to paraphrase the veteran teacher's recommendation in a nonjudgmental way, which serves to acknowledge the idea, and then states, "Two members feel the team should move forward using a copy of last year's unit plans." Everyone nods, and the coach continues to probe for specificity by asking questions that require the veteran teacher to reflect on why she deems the unit successful and describe why it would benefit the current group of students. There is a brief pause between each question, allowing other members time to reflect.

The veteran teacher reflects on the success of the previous year's summative assessment results and remembers that the results were weaker than originally expected. Her reflection spurs conversation among the other team members as they compare last year's unit plan with the strengths and needs of this year's students.

The coach also is aware that not all team members have shared ideas and invites everyone to put his or her ideas on the table. The conversation continues among the team members until they reach consensus on a revised unit plan everyone agrees would best meet the needs of their current students.

At the end of the meeting, the coach and team take a few minutes to reflect on the planning process. In this particular meeting, the coach highlighted the use of paraphrasing, probing for specificity, pausing, and putting ideas on the table. The debriefing gave teachers an opportunity to share how they felt the team had functioned and provided the coach an opportunity to speak more about his intentional moves related to the seven norms of collaboration.

Example Two: Elementary Team

An elementary team of five teachers has been working together and collaborating at a very high level for the past two years. The team learned about the seven norms of collaboration and had successfully incorporated them into their planning process. They are committed to making the seven norms a habit of their professional practice.

The team begins each team meeting with the same routine: they quickly review the norms posted on the table and choose to pay close attention to one norm they believe will enhance the team's productivity. The team decides to focus on pausing during their discussions, acknowledging that working together for so many years has caused team members to almost be able to finish each other's sentences, which leads to the tendency to interrupt and talk over one another.

Throughout the meeting, the coach helps team members hold one another accountable to the norm of pausing and allowing some time to think after members share ideas. They also pay attention to the impact pausing has on their ability to gather their thoughts and clarify their own thinking before sharing any feedback with their colleagues.

At the end of the meeting, each teacher acknowledges that the intentional focus on pausing has helped everyone be more reflective. The heightened attention to pausing and its impact on the team also creates a new level of trust and respect since all members feel like they have contributed to the conversation.

Coaching a Shift to a Collective Focus

Laura Lipton and Bruce Wellman (2012) write the following about the shift from individual to collective focus.

> Moving from *my students* and *my work* to *our students* and *our work* requires clear purpose, safe structures, and compelling data that present vivid images of the effects of teachers' work. This shift from individual perspective to collective perspective is the heart of collaborative inquiry . . . (p. 2)

Additionally, Gen-Ling Chang-Wells and Gordon Wells (1997) share that language is the main "tool for collaborative remembering, thinking, problem solving and acting" (p. 149). A coach must cultivate language that promotes collective inquiry.

The adage, "How we talk is as important as what we talk about," resonates with those who support the collective-inquiry process. To maximize the benefits of collective inquiry, coaches support the development of language and questioning routines that are open ended and include tentative language. A coach helps teams recognize the value of exploring new ideas, balancing participation, seeking understanding, and offering up ideas. Development of these routines leads to long lasting habits that keep conversations focused on possibilities, foster trust, and diminish conflict.

Garmston and Wellman (2013) note that "learning at its root is a questioning process and successful collaboration embraces the patterns and practices of inquiry" (p. 42). After all, if questioning isn't present and one member of a team owns all the sharing, thinking, and learning, it isn't collective, nor is it inquiry, and it sure isn't effective.

To improve learning and development of shared knowledge, proficient teams intentionally incorporate questions that promote the outcomes they are seeking. Marilee C. Goldberg (1998) states that "because questions are intrinsically related to action, they spark and direct attention, perception, energy, and effort, and so are at the heart of the evolving forms that our lives assume" (p. 3).

Figure 3.2 is a sample of the shift in language that coaches can promote to create conditions for the collective learning and inquiry process to take hold. These examples change the noun from singular to plural form (for example, *strategy* to *strategies*), and the question incorporates tentative language that invites participation (such as *might* and *possible*). These examples illustrate a shift from identification of a definitive answer (singular focus) to multiple possibilities to investigate (collective focus).

Shift From Individual Focus	To Collective Focus
What strategy will you use?	What strategies might we explore?
How do you explain this result?	What might be some possible explanations for this result?
What is the reason for this success?	What might be the reasons for this success?

Figure 3.2: Shift in language from individual to collective focus.

Figure 3.3 offers additional stems that promote the use of tentative vocabulary. When teams increase their use of tentative language in their collaborative planning around the four critical questions of a PLC, it promotes further inquiry and exploration of new ideas.

Instead of . . .	Try Using . . .
• What is the solution? • It is clear that . . . • What is the best idea? • The next step is . . . • Everyone knows that . . . • Obviously . . . • We definitely need to . . . • We must . . . • It is . . .	• Another possibility . . . • We might consider . . . • A hunch I have . . . • What might . . . • Other options can include . . . • Appears to . . . • Suggests that . . . • Seems to . . .

Figure 3.3: Tentative vocabulary stems.

Visit ***go.SolutionTree.com/PLCbooks*** *for a free reproducible version of this figure.*

Coaching to Promote Inquiry Through Questioning

Modeling and monitoring the inquiry questions teams use in conjunction with the PLC process is another intentional move a coach can use with collaborative teams. Modeling provides examples of the types of questions connected to the PLC process that teams might consider and highlights their specific use within the context of a team meeting. Figure 3.4 (page 52) shows examples of inquiry-type questions related to four categories that align to effective team processes.

Inquiry Category	Open-Ended Structure With Tentative and Plural Language
Exploring Possibility	• As we consider the data in front of us, what might be some priorities to consider? • What are some of our perspectives on instructional practices that weren't as effective as we had hoped? • What other approaches could we consider? • Considering our goal, what instructional practices do research highlight that hold promise? • I'm wondering, what strategy could we test? Are their others to consider? • What assumptions underlie our rationale for prioritizing this as a next step? • Based on our identified goal, what data points shall we consider for helping us define success? • What are some areas of strength in our instructional practice that we should celebrate? • What are other factors that might inhibit us from reaching our identified goal? • What do areas of further investigation seem to be?
Balancing Participation	• We haven't heard from everyone on the team. Who else would like to add their thoughts? • ______, what are you thinking? • I'm curious about what the others around the table are thinking. • It is important we understand multiple points of view. Who else can add to what has been discussed already?
Seeking to Understand	• Can you elaborate on your thinking about why this strategy didn't seem to impact learning as much as you hoped? • Say more about the hunches you have about why that strategy worked well for so many of your students. • Which solution would you advocate for and why? • What are the connections you notice between the outcomes we hope to achieve and the research on the topic? • Can you tell me a little more about your ideas on the research you read? • I'm intrigued by the application of our new learning to our upcoming unit. Can you elaborate? • Based on our results, what are some things we may do differently next time?
Encouraging Participation	• How might we ______? • I am thinking about it like this ______. What are your thoughts? • I have an idea to consider. May I share it? • Might there be another possible way we could . . . ? Or think about . . . ? • I've been thinking about ______ here's an idea.

Figure 3.4: Inquiry-type questions for effective team processes.

In order to build automaticity with inquiry-based questions, coaches and teams can also make a list of questions they typically use in their collaborative team meetings, and then redraft them to be open ended. This helps teams interact firsthand with the language structure, so they can better replicate the pattern in their interactions with each other. There are also numerous inquiry-based protocols available online that provide a resource for teams. A coach can review the protocols in advance and let teams easily peruse the various options available to reach consensus on those they would like to pilot. Matching the right inquiry protocol with a team's style creates ownership in the tools.

Additionally, teams may choose to set a goal to practice using a predetermined inquiry question that is relevant to a specific outcome of an upcoming meeting. This goal-oriented approach precipitates an action orientation. To monitor the goal, many teams have found success designating one member of the team to be a process observer while also fulfilling his or her role as a teammate in the PLC process. After teams practice embedding the inquiry question into their collaborative meeting, the process observer provides feedback to the team on the impact the question had on his or her overall effectiveness and outcomes. In effect, the process observer takes on the role of team member and coach as he or she supports the inquiry goal the team wanted to achieve. This results in an authentic way to build the capacity for teams to monitor and coach and improve their own practice internally.

In the beginning, coaches and teams might find that collective inquiry feels contrived and prescriptive, almost artificial. But, like any new process, time and practice will lead to development of a new routine. Then, over time, a coach's hands-on role in guiding collective inquiry should decrease. A coach's work is to build the capacity of the team so that the team functions independently at a high level with collective inquiry.

Incorporating questions alone will not change team meetings. However, when coaches and teams infuse a shift in these patterns of questions and use of language into practice, teams begin to thrive as a result of enhanced patterns of interaction among all team members.

Coaching to Set a Realistic Vision

High-impact coaches choose to combine collective inquiry with an action orientation and a focus on results knowing it is a powerful continuous improvement model to help teachers become more effective.

Coaches committed to improving PLCs recognize that developing routines is a process that is cultivated over time. Formation of productive habits and automaticity are the goals. A coach must consider how to communicate to stakeholders that establishing a shared skill set among teachers takes time and energy. Equally important, they must acknowledge small successes as teams succeed and take time to debrief attempts that do not hit the mark. This encouragement will create an arena for teams to experiment with and test their new routines.

In the following section, we explore how coaching inquiry routines and habits is more effective when teams use the inquiry SIG as their reference point and the pathways tool to monitor their progress.

Using the Inquiry SIG and Pathways Tools

The inquiry SIG in figure 3.5, with its anchor statements, indicators, and descriptors, provides a flight plan that is beneficial in helping coaches and teams understand their current state of collective inquiry as well as determine next possible best steps for a team. Connecting feedback and support to the tool will help propel teams forward to stronger inquiry-based collaboration.

Anchor Statement		
Educators build shared knowledge by clarifying the questions that a group will explore together. They engage in collective inquiry into more effective practices by examining both external evidence (such as research) and internal evidence (which teachers are getting the best results). They also build shared knowledge regarding the reality of the current practices and conditions in their schools or districts.		
Beyond Proficient	**Proficient**	**Below Proficient**
Teams work interdependently to prioritize and monitor goals focused on learning for all students to which they are mutually accountable. Teams have established collective commitments. Team dialogue is infused with collective language such as "we" instead of "me." Teams readily challenge current practice and embrace next practice. They ask, "Why not?" rather than "Why should we?" Teams naturally pose questions in collaborative meetings to invite deep dialogue, explore thinking, and to specify thinking.	Teams work interdependently to set and monitor goals focused on learning for all students. Team dialogue shifts between collective language such as "we" and an individualized view of "I." Teams embrace logical safe next steps with some apprehension. Teams value posing questions that tend to be more surface level in nature. They may or may not push on thinking and practice.	Teams meet and coplan to share practices and resources. Teachers use their own discretion and can choose to continue to rely on their own past practice and goals if they disagree. Team dialogue is singular in nature and is based on pronouns where an "I" or "me" viewpoint is evident. There is preference and reliance on historical instructional practice, actions, and teaming. Teams rely on congenial interactions. There is limited or no opportunity to challenge or question.

Beyond Proficient	Proficient	Below Proficient
Teams use language that encourages participation and promotes choice and safety by incorporating plural forms and tentative language. Team success to benefit students is the goal.	Teams use language that encourages participation. At times, the inconsistent use of plural forms and tentative language tends to limit options and participation.	Team language is driven by individual statements and perspectives. Individuals try to convince others and an alternative point of view is rarely explored. Winning is viewed as success.
Teams use data to challenge underlying assumptions and the status quo. Teams are collegial and embrace cognitive dissonance within the PLC process.	Teams use data to make instructional decisions that may be limited in scope. Teams function as a unit and rely, at times, on congenial interactions.	Team decisions are based on personal assumptions and past instructional practice. Use of data is limited or not accessed during decision making.
Team members build shared knowledge by blending perspectives and balancing participation. They share ideas and seek to understand other viewpoints.	Teams value building shared knowledge. At times, certain viewpoints still dominate the dialogue, limiting opportunities to learn from one another.	Teams are dominated by individuals or small groups. Participation from all stakeholders is diminished. Certain individual perspectives hold more clout.
Teams use student data to draw conclusions, define principles, and they commit to apply new learning to unique, unpredictable situations.	Teams examine student data and reflect on effective instructional practice. Team application of new learning is inconsistent.	Teams compare results to historical trends and rarely adjust instruction. They tend to rationalize student results to circumstances beyond their control.
Teams make decisions based on common learning to commit to implement next instructional practice.	Teams commit to the next instructional practice but follow through to implementation may not be consistent.	Teams function with limited or no collective commitment. Team processes haven't been fully developed.

Figure 3.5: Inquiry SIG.

*Visit **go.SolutionTree.com/PLCbooks** for a free reproducible version of this figure.*

A coach can also support teams by using the pathways tool for inquiry (figure 3.6, page 56). The tool incorporates a series of hierarchical questions that help both the coach and the team understand where the next level of support might take place.

The four routines figure 3.6 (page 56) details are foundational to inquiry in the PLC process. By embedding all four routines (exploring possibilities, putting ideas on the table, balancing participation, and seeking to understand), a team will naturally function at a higher level. This is a catalyst to develop a coaching culture where inquiry thrives.

Exploring Possibility	Putting Ideas on the Table	Balancing Participation	Seeking to Understand
What do you notice about collective team outcomes? How does the team prioritize their next area of study? How does the team enter conversations that allow for dissonance and challenge? What are the intentional moves a team makes to identify effective practices leading to next steps?	What do you notice about team interactions? To what extent is there a team culture of respect, inclusion, and risk taking? How can you make the team members aware of their interactions so that all members feel safe, valued, and respected for their individual viewpoints? What are the collective commitments of the team? Who is responsible for monitoring team culture so all participants share ideas?	What do you notice about team participation? What is the frequency of equal participation amongst team members? What protocols are in place that ensure balanced participation from all team members? Who will monitor participation in the future? When and how will the team reflect on team participation?	What do you notice as you listen to team members question one another? What is the frequency of tentative and plural language during team dialogue? What scaffolds or modeling needs to occur in order for the team to understand the benefits of plural and tentative language? Who will monitor the use of plural and tentative language? When and how will the team members reflect on their use of plural and tentative language?

Figure 3.6: Pathways tool for inquiry.

Visit ***go.SolutionTree.com/PLCbooks*** *for a free reproducible version of this figure.*

For example, when a team is collaboratively planning, the coach (principal, coach, or team leader) can ask the open-ended inquiry pathway questions to help guide the team to consider a different approach and celebrate progress. When a coach poses a question, it provides the opportunity for the team to reflect and ask for clarification, thus creating a teachable moment.

Lastly, as collective efficacy is developed with the Inquiry Pathways, a team can monitor its own progress and identify gaps that might be hindering progress.

Moving Forward

A coach must fundamentally believe that the essential element of collective inquiry is not another initiative, but rather an expectation about how faculty members engage with and learn from one another. Not only is the team stronger because members work as a unit and establish rapport and trust, but they begin to know that they are influencing student learning together.

The development of the habits highlighted in this chapter will set collaborative teams up for success as they engage in the essential PLC element of continuous improvement detailed in the next chapter.

Summary

- Collective inquiry is commonplace in a variety of organizations, including high-performing PLCs.
- The process of collective inquiry allows teams to build shared knowledge that ultimately will benefit student learning.
- A coach's choice of language is essential to creating a collective focus for a team.
- Collective inquiry is a byproduct of the questions teams investigate in the PLC process.
- Coaching collective inquiry is anchored in the seven norms of collaboration.
- The use of the SIG and pathways tool supports collective inquiry.

Reflection Questions

A coach plays an instrumental role in cultivating the conditions that are necessary for collective inquiry to thrive. As you reflect on the content of this chapter, consider the following four questions.

1. What are the challenges to promoting a climate that is conducive to collective inquiry in your school?
2. What are your strengths as a coach related to collective inquiry?
3. What are your vulnerabilities?
4. What is one skill that you will focus on to increase your efficacy and impact on teams?

CHAPTER 4

Staying Restless—The Impact of Continuous Improvement

Inherent to a PLC are a persistent disquiet with the status quo and a constant search for a better way to achieve goals and accomplish the purpose of the organization.

—RICHARD DUFOUR

The most successful schools are learning organizations where everyone is continuously seeking out new and better ways of doing things. These schools operate with the understanding that the key to improved learning for students is a commitment to continuous improvement on the part of the adults that serve them.

Very few of us, whether in education or any other profession, work the way we did ten or fifteen years ago, and the rate at which new and better ways of doing things are discovered is accelerating every day. As an example of the importance of this element of the PLC process, consider the stories of Zenith Television and Blockbuster Video.

Many of us grew up watching a Zenith television. For years, Zenith dominated the domestic market with the big, round tube televisions that were considered the industry's standard of excellence. Eventually, Japanese manufactures like Sony introduced solid state technology and the traditional vacuum-tube-based television, long considered to be best practice, became obsolete, replaced with the next generation of televisions.

Likewise, Blockbuster was once the dominant retailer in the video rental market and was also considered to be an example of best practice for that industry. In 2000, the CEO of Netflix approached Blockbuster with an offer to sell his company for fifty million dollars (Chong, 2015). After considering the opportunity to move into the streaming video market, Blockbuster rejected the Netflix offer and decided to stick with their existing business model (brick and mortar stores filled with videos) that had worked so well for so many years. Just ten years later in 2010, Blockbuster declared bankruptcy and by 2018 there was only *one* Blockbuster store left in operation (Horton, 2018). Over the same time period, Netflix grew to be a thirty-two billion dollar company and replaced Blockbuster as the model of best practice in the industry (Chong, 2015).

Similar cycles have occurred in auto manufacturing, mobile telephones, and a host of other industries. One might wonder about why organizations lose their edge; it may be complacency, a lack of investment in research and development, or simply bad management, but whatever the reason, Zenith and Blockbuster did not (or could not) respond to new ways of doing things and their version of best practice became outdated. The lesson educators can learn from these corporate examples is that in a rapidly changing environment, organizations must commit to continuous improvement or risk becoming obsolete.

A Continuum of Professional Practice

Today's educators work in a rapidly changing environment, and while teachers strive every day to engage in best practice, ours is a learning profession and, thus, the definition of what is best practice today will inevitably become past practice at some future point. As teachers work together to discover new ways of doing things, practices that were once considered best practice naturally evolve into next practice (the next generation of best practice). It's helpful to view the different levels of professional practice along a continuum from malpractice to next practice (see figure 4.1). We examine these levels—malpractice, safe practice, best practice, and next practice—in the sections that follow.

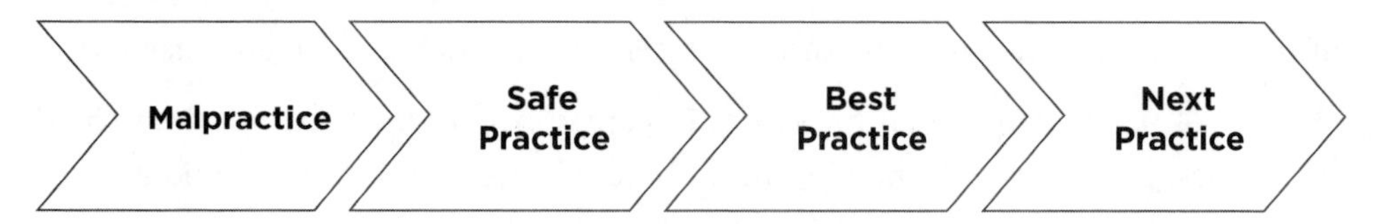

Figure 4.1: Continuum of professional practice.

Malpractice

When teachers implement practices or support policies and procedures that have been disproven or replaced by more effective and efficient ways of doing things, they are engaging in a form of educational malpractice. For example, in 2018 there are still schools where attitude, effort, and behavior are all mixed into the grade; grading criteria are unclear to students; and zeros are averaged into a series of summative assessments. All of these practices have been discredited for nearly twenty years, yet some schools continue to hang onto their antiquated grading traditions (Guskey, 2000b; Marzano, 2000; Reeves, 2004).

Safe Practice

Teams engage in safe practice when they support policies, practices, and procedures that protect the status quo. In most cases, safe practice was best practice at one time but has since been replaced with approaches that are more effective. Safe practice is not controversial, it is often built around a sense of comfort or predictability, and is justified as "just the way things are done around here." Examples of safe grading practice might include averaging scores from a series of different assessments; grading everything regardless of when or why it was completed; and while attitude, effort, and behavior are mixed into the grade, teachers use separate feedback structures during the reporting process.

Best Practice

Best practices are those practices, policies, and procedures that reflect current thinking, have been proven in literature, and are supported by evidence. Examples of best practice in grading would incorporate grading criteria that are clear to all, reflect a blend of learning goals and performance standards, combine evidence from a variety of formative and summative assessments, and emphasize the most recent level of student learning when calculating the final grade.

Next Practice

Next practice—or the next generation of best practice—are those ideas that we may not yet fully understand but recognize as opportunities to push the boundaries of teaching and learning. Next practice in grading would use evidence of learning—as opposed to the exclusive reliance on assessment results—aligned to standards and targets that are criterion referenced, proficiency based, and reflect a student's current level of learning.

Keeping up with the accelerating pace of change and innovation may seem daunting, but the most effective schools know that the best way to ensure teacher teams are able to respond to new ideas or new ways of doing things is to embrace continuous improvement as a habit of professional practice. In a PLC, a team's professional practice is getting better or worse; it rarely stays the same. In an effective PLC, teams are constantly seeking out the next generation of best practice.

According to Todd White, superintendent of schools for Blue Valley School District in Overland Park, Kansas, "Best practice allows the system to do what it does efficiently and effectively. Next practice increases an organization's capability to do the things it has never done before" (personal communication, June 1, 2016).

Reflection and Current Practice

One of the first things practitioners notice about the PLC process is that teachers are constantly reflecting on their current practice. Curiosity and a persistent disquiet with the status quo are two characteristics at the heart of continuous improvement. When both of these characteristics are present on a collaborative team, we describe that team as being *restless* about their practice. The very best teams maintain a *relentless state of restlessness* around their practice and are constantly working to improve.

The continuous improvement process begins when teachers ask themselves questions like, Is there a better way to deliver this lesson? or, How might we improve this assessment? The team may decide that at this time, what they are doing *is* the most effective and efficient way, or, they may decide that they should consider an alternative approach. Regardless of what they decide, *asking* the question can be just as important as *answering* the question.

Continuous improvement, an essential element of the PLC process, is one of the best ways to maintain high levels of professional practice and a hallmark of highly effective teams but, continuous improvement requires patience and commitment until it becomes a habit of professional practice and what principals and coaches need to understand is there is nothing *continuous* about school improvement efforts if teachers do not have an opportunity to develop the tasks, routines, and habits of professional practice. As Rick DuFour (2004) notes:

> The goal is not simply to learn a new strategy, but instead to create conditions for a perpetual learning environment in which innovation and experimentation are viewed not as tasks or projects to be completed but as ways of conducting day to day business—forever. (p. 5)

The Carnegie Foundation defines continuous improvement as "the act of integrating quality improvement into the daily work of individuals in the system" (Park, Hironaka, Carver, & Nordstrum, 2013, p. 5). Elgart (2017) defines continuous improvement as "an embedded behavior within the culture of a school that constantly focuses on the conditions, processes, and practices that will improve teaching and learning" (p. 55). For our purposes, we will adopt the language of AllThingsPLC (2016), which defines continuous improvement as, "The ongoing cycle of planning, doing, checking, and acting designed to improve results—constantly" (p. 2).

The term *continuous improvement* originated in the private sector during the 1930s and gained widespread popularity during the 1950s as a result of Edwards Deming's work with Japanese manufacturing after World War II. Deming introduced the Plan Do Study Act (PDSA) cycle, which many schools and districts have modified and adapted. Since the original introduction of PDSA, there have been many variations, but all share the same principles.

The PDSA Cycle

Teachers working in a PLC naturally engage in some form of continuous improvement on a regular basis; it is part of the PLC process. AllThingsPLC (2016) describes what continuous improvement looks like in a PLC by explaining:

> This cycle includes gathering evidence of current levels of student learning, developing strategies and ideas to build on strengths and address weaknesses in that learning, implementing those strategies and ideas, analyzing the impact of the changes to discover what was effective and what was not, and applying the new knowledge in the next cycle of continuous improvement. (p. 2)

While most teams practice parts of the cycle on a daily basis, few complete the entire cycle as part of their team's collaborative routines.

The PDSA cycle is a useful framework for understanding the basic concepts of continuous improvement. It is not designed to produce change as a result of a single big, breakthrough moment; instead, the power of the PDSA cycle is in the repetition of a series of short-term cycles of change. The typical PDSA cycle consists of four stages (Gorenflo & Moran, 2010; Langley et al., 2009, as cited in Park et al., 2013).

- **Plan:** A team studies a problem that needs to be solved, collects baseline data on that problem, elaborates potential solution to that problem, and develops an action plan.
- **Do:** The team implements its action plan, collects data on its intervention, and records developments.
- **Study:** The team gauges the success of the intervention by comparing baseline and new data, analyzes results, and documents lessons learned.
- **Act:** The team determines what to do with its results. Depending on the success of its intervention, the team may choose to adopt, adapt, or abandon the tested solution.

Plan

A cycle of continuous improvement begins as teams identify a problem of practice during the planning stage. The coach's role at this stage is to help teams identify opportunities to improve their practice. The team's problem of practice is based on data, feedback, or other evidence of learning gathered from observations or samples of student work and common assessments. After reviewing the data, the team decides what aspect of their work they could improve and proposes a change. This first stage of the cycle ends as the team predicts what impact the change or changes may have on student learning.

Do

In the doing stage, teams plan and conduct a small-scale pilot of the proposed change. Teachers may choose to work on something as simple as helping students identify text features or as complex as designing a schoolwide system for providing more time and support to students. The task at this stage is to implement, measure, and assess whether the change improved student learning. A coach helps teams identify which data the team will need to gather in order to measure impact, interpret the data, decide whether the change improved student learning, and if so, by how much.

Study

During the study stage of the PDSA cycle, a coach helps teams describe and document precisely what happened and why. In this stage, coaches often find that protocols are beneficial as teams fine tune their understanding of the impact of the change. These conversations are focused on ways the team might apply what they have learned to improve teaching and learning in their school.

Act

Act is the final stage of the PDSA cycle. The PDSA cycle ends with a coach helping the team identify what aspects of the change members will retain, refine, or replace before moving on to the next iteration of the PDSA cycle, which might focus on a new aspect of the team's professional practice. Or the team might drill deeper and extend the learning they generated with the current PDSA cycle, just at a more sophisticated level.

Examining the PDSA cycle as part of a case study can help those who coach teams appreciate how each of the components work together as part of a single process. To understand how the PDSA cycle helps teams improve, reflect on the story of one elementary team as it made a series of small, incremental changes to improve the delivery of interventions.

The PDSA Cycle in Action

In one elementary school, each teacher has a thirty-minute WINN (What I Need Now) time built into his or her schedule four days per week. During WINN time, teachers keep their own students in their homeroom and deliver Tier 2 interventions to students who are not proficient in reading, writing, and mathematics. Despite their best efforts and the commitment of a dedicated time for interventions, the team does not see the expected improvements in student achievement. Using the PDSA cycle as a guide, the coach works with the team to identify a problem of practice (How would changing the intervention schedule impact student learning?) and generate some alternative ways of organizing WINN time.

In the first round of the PDSA cycle, teachers decide to maintain the previous practice of working with students assigned to their homeroom, but instead of intervening simultaneously in all three subjects every day, the team chooses to concentrate on one subject per day: Monday, reading; Tuesday, writing; Wednesday, mathematics; and they leave Thursday as a flex day. Individual teachers then determine the subject of Thursday's interventions based on their students' needs.

The team makes the change, gathers data on how designating a different subject each day impacts student learning, and reconvenes three weeks later to review their findings. While the team agrees WINN time was more organized, teachers feel there are still too many students who continue to need help with too many different skills all at the same time. The team decides to continue making adjustments to WINN time in an effort to get better results.

Before the start of the second cycle, teachers give students a common assessment to identify specific areas where they are experiencing difficulty and need more help. Students continue to remain in their homerooms, but teachers organize them into small groups based on the specific skills the assessment data identified as lacking. After three weeks of trying the new system to organize the students, the consensus is this new structure actually makes WINN more frustrating, and there is talk of dropping WINN altogether—it is just too complicated. The coach encourages the team to continue tweaking the way they deliver WINN time in an effort to get it right.

In the third round of PDSA, teachers continue to focus on a different subject each day of the week but begin regrouping students across the grade level based on the skills rather than by a student's homeroom assignment. The results of this round of the PDSA cycle are encouraging. The team sees evidence that the groupings are more efficient, and, while this approach to organizing WINN requires an extra commitment of time to organize, regroup, and transition the students into groups based on skills, teachers report that the scope of the interventions are more targeted, and the level of student achievement has improved.

The commitment to an ongoing process of continuous improvement is how teams improve their practice. As this quick case study demonstrates, the PDSA cycle is an effective tool to promote continuous improvement; it supports a team's long-term improvement efforts by promoting a series of short-term cycles of change.

A Long-Term Commitment

Continuous improvement is the means to an end, a way to accomplish a goal; it is not an end in and of itself. Teachers understand that the process of continuous improvement is powerful because it is so deeply connected to learning. Principals and coaches should not ask how well the process of continuous improvement is going, but rather how the process of continuous improvement is helping teams reach their goals and fulfill their mission of high levels of learning for all. This daily commitment to continuous improvement—of teams being *relentlessly restless* around their professional practice—is one of the essential elements of a high-performing PLC.

To be successful, continuous improvement requires a lasting commitment, and it is imperative that leaders not only maintain a commitment to long-term school SMART goals and improvement strategies, but also that they coach teams in developing their own commitment to short-term improvement cycles. Too many believe continuous improvement is synonymous with the never-ending introduction of new strategies, standards, or technology, but that kind of approach to school improvement does nothing to improve teaching and learning. Those in coaching roles must be patient and nurture the process. When using the PDSA cycle, coaches should encourage teams to adopt a "think big, but start small" approach and seek out opportunities for quick wins. The truth is, "The only way for quality improvement work to be truly continuous is if it is woven into the fabric of the daily work that individuals are constantly doing" (Park et al., p. 5).

During a training in Klein, Texas, Donny Osborn of Klein Independent School District told a story of a principal who had once asked him, "How do I know if teams are stuck in a rut or finding their groove?" Osborne responded that "the difference between a rut and a groove is how long you stay in the same spot" (D. Osborn, personal communication, June 22, 2018). Being stuck in a rut and finding your groove can look a lot alike, but the answer to this question lies in the degree to which teams have embraced continuous improvement as a habit of their professional practice.

When collaborative teams stop investigating new ideas and become rigid in their thinking, they become stagnant. When teams get stagnant, they stop learning. When teams stop learning, they get stuck in a rut, their performance declines, and they become less and less effective. On the other hand, when collaborative teams are curious about their professional practice and resilient in their thinking, they build momentum. When teams build momentum, they improve. When teams improve, they find their groove, their performance is enhanced, and they make steady and sustained progress.

The answer to this principal's question is to reflect on Osborn's observation and ensure teams keep learning, growing, and improving. The best way to ensure that happens, and to make certain teachers avoid getting stuck in a rut and instead find their groove, is to embrace continuous improvement. Sounds easy, but without coaching, teams struggle to make continuous improvement a habit of their professional practice. The SIG and pathways for this essential element assist coaches in moving teams forward in their practice.

Using the Continuous-Improvement SIG and Pathways Tools

The Continuous Improvement SIG in figure 4.2, with its anchor statement, indicators, and descriptors, provides a flight plan that is beneficial in helping coaches and teams understand their current state of continuous improvement as well as determine next possible best steps for a team. Connecting feedback and support to the tool will help propel teams forward to stronger collaboratively determined next practices.

Anchor Statement		
Teacher teams are constantly engaged in an ongoing process of planning, doing, checking, and taking actions designed to improve results.		
Beyond Proficient	**Proficient**	**Below Proficient**
The team embraces and regularly seeks out opportunities to use the PDSA cycle as a way to improve their practice. When teams engage in the PDSA cycle, the effort is complete and considered to be "just part of the way we do business." The team has created routines and the PDSA cycle has become a habit of their professional practice.	The team is willing, when asked, to use the PDSA cycle as a means of improving their practice. When teams engage in the PDSA cycle, the effort is mechanical and takes a great deal of effort. The team is aware of and values continuous improvement but has yet to incorporate it as a routine process on their team.	The team is reluctant, even when asked, to use the PDSA cycle as a means of improving their practice. When teams engage in the PDSA cycle, they often skip steps or leave them out of the process. The team views the continuous improvement process as a compliance activity.

Figure 4.2: Continuous improvement SIG.

*Visit **go.SolutionTree.com/PLCbooks** for a free reproducible version of this figure.*

A coach can also support teams by using the pathways tool for continuous improvement (figure 4.3, page 68). The tool incorporates a series of hierarchical questions that help both the coach and the team understand where the next level of support is needed. Consider this tool and questions a catalyst to the coaching process. For example, if a team wants to move from the proficient to the beyond proficient level on the Continuous Improvement SIG, the pathways tool can serve as the outline for the team to work through as members decide how they might improve their PLC practice.

Plan: Identify a Problem of Practice	Do: Conduct Small Scale Pilot of Plan	Study: Understand What Happened and Why	Act: Determine Next Steps
What is the problem that needs to be solved? What data do we have regarding the problem we are attempting to solve? What data will the team need to collect regarding the problem we are trying to solve? What are some potential solutions that the team might consider? What steps will we include in the action plan to solve the problem?	What logistics are associated with the implementation of the action plan? (Identify the who, what, when, and where of the action.) What will we use to collect and organize the data resulting from implementation of the plan? What will we use to record and analyze the data resulting from implementation of the plan?	How will we analyze the data we gathered from the implementation of the plan? What will be the basis of comparing pre- and post-data in order to measure the impact of the plan? What protocols should we consider using to make our work more effective and efficient? What new ideas or insights did we gain from piloting the plan?	What evidence did we find that would suggest we should adopt, adapt, or abandon this plan? What are the next steps might we take to solve the problem?

Figure 4.3: Pathways for continuous improvement.
Visit ***go.SolutionTree.com/PLCbooks*** *for a free reproducible version of this figure.*

Moving Forward

Continuous improvement is one of the essential elements of the PLC process. It is critical that teams engage in short cycles of improvement in order to ensure their practice is both effective and efficient. While the process of continuous improvement is ongoing, the most effective teams are conscientious, even meticulous, about turning their new learning and insight into actionable steps. The next chapter addresses the importance of an action orientation in a high-performing PLC.

Summary

- The most successful schools are learning organizations where everyone is continuously seeking out new and better ways of doing things.
- In a rapidly changing environment, organizations must commit to continuous improvement or risk becoming obsolete.
- Curiosity and a persistent disquiet with the status quo are two characteristics at the heart of continuous improvement.

- There is nothing *continuous* about school improvement if teachers do not have an opportunity to develop the tasks and routines into habits of professional practice.
- The PDSA cycle is a useful framework for understanding the basic concepts of continuous improvement.
- Continuous improvement supports long-term improvement by promoting a series of short-term cycles of change.

Reflection Questions

A coach plays an instrumental role in cultivating the conditions that are necessary for continuous improvement to thrive. As you reflect on the content of this chapter, consider the following three questions.

1. Does continuous improvement represent a mindset teams must have, a series of steps teams must follow, or a combination of both?
2. Which is more important—embracing the mindset of continuous improvement or following the steps of the PDSA cycle? Explain your answer.
3. Think of a time when a team you were a member of used the PDSA cycle. Explain whether the team's efforts were successful and why.

CHAPTER 5

Being Urgent—The Value of an Action Orientation

> *Organizations that turn knowledge into action by not letting talk substitute for behavior are relentlessly action oriented.*
>
> **—JEFFERY PFEFFER AND ROBERT SUTTON**

We find examples of ways that complex systems, both inside and outside education, respond to our fast-paced, ever changing world with an orientation towards action. For example, in sports, athletes must play the game, run the race, and so on—they must participate in their sport. Quality training and preparation, eating right, and studying the game help athletes perform at higher levels, but those actions are no substitute for participating in their sport and competing. Athletes learn by doing and improve with coaching.

In medicine, residents learn new procedures following the sequence of "hear one, see one, do one" (Pfeffer & Sutton 2000, p. 23). The learning process begins with explanation and understanding, moves to observation, and ends with actually operating on a patient all while receiving guidance and coaching from an attending physician during the surgery; an action orientation is an accepted part of the learning process in medicine.

In schools, an action orientation is both a motor and a motivator. When teacher teams act in purposeful ways, and as they learn more than they knew before, they put their new knowledge into action. Pfeffer and Sutton (2000) believe that "you cannot gain experience and make as many meaningful connections without doing . . . taking action will generate experience from which you can learn" (p. 6).

Action orientation consists of equal parts action and urgency and could be defined as *taking action with urgency*. DuFour, DuFour, Eaker, & Many (2006) state the following about PLCs and action orientation.

> Members of PLCs are action oriented: they move quickly to turn aspirations into actions and visions into reality. They understand that the most powerful learning always occurs in a context of taking action, and they value engagement and experience as the most effective teachers. (p. 4)

Taking action on behalf of students is a good beginning, but anyone can take action. What distinguishes an action orientation in a PLC is that team actions are not arbitrary or random; they are deliberate and purposeful. When teams in a PLC act, they act in ways that are intentionally designed to ensure high levels of learning for all.

Teams in a PLC also act with a sense of urgency; they act with resolve and determination that places student learning as the team's highest priority. These teams move from looking at data or evidence, to identifying alternative strategies and techniques, to changing their classroom practices in ways that create higher levels of learning for their students—and they do it *now*. Coaches help teams to be action oriented when they encourage them to take action while engaging in the right work.

In the seminal book *Learning by Doing: A Handbook for Professional Learning Communities at Work* (DuFour et al., 2016), the authors emphasize the importance of an action orientation.

> Perhaps the greatest insight we have gained in our work with school districts in the United States and throughout the world is that organizations that take the plunge and actually begin *doing* the work of a PLC to develop their capacity to help all students learn at high levels far more effectively than schools that spend years *preparing* to become PLCs through reading or even training. (p. 23)

Michael Fullan (2008) concurs and adds, "Learning on the job, day after day, is the work" (p. 86). "It is learning by purposeful doing that counts most" (Fullan & Quinn, 2016, p. 21). Henry Mintzberg's (2004) observation about training leaders applies here as well. He suggests that successful leadership "is as much about doing in order to think as thinking in order to do" (p. 10), and he argues that deep learning requires experience, which requires taking action.

What's clear from Fullan and Mintzberg's observations is that participating in more workshops, book studies, and lectures will not get teams where they need to be. We know that people learn best by applying their knowledge and reflecting on the experience. Coaching teams to more productive levels of practice by doing the work (with a focus on the big ideas and the four critical questions of a PLC) has produced significant improvements in teaching and learning. As Richard DuFour (2015) describes:

> Researchers from around the world have confirmed the power of the PLC process. It has been endorsed by virtually all the professional organizations for educators in the United States. It is consistent with recommendations for best practice from organizational theorists outside of education. Each of its various elements is grounded in a solid research base. (pp. 81–82)

Connecting Learning to the Work

One of the best ways to promote an action orientation is to ask teams to produce products that are connected to the work. DuFour et al. (2016) describe this approach as "one of the purposeful steps leaders can take in creating a professional learning community" (p. 74). When teams create products such as rubrics, proficiency scales, common formative assessments, and graphic organizers, they deepen their understanding of the underlying foundation of concepts or practices. The simple act of producing a product has been known to propel teams into action.

During their early years of the PLC journey, the faculty and staff of Kildeer Countryside Community Consolidated School District 96 in Buffalo Grove, Illinois, were struggling to design a schoolwide and systematic intervention plan for their schools. Despite their best efforts, the administrative team could not reach consensus on what a plan for schoolwide and systematic interventions would look like. The team members agreed that if they could not write it down, the plan didn't really exist, and so after an especially spirited conversation, principals were asked to work with their teachers and other principals to create a parent brochure describing the plan and all the different resources that were available to students who were not yet proficient. The brochure was to include an explanation of the resources, actions, and commitments each level in the district was willing to make in order to ensure all students would learn.

A new sense of urgency was evident once teams were given the charge and a deadline for completion. Principals created an action research project and began to work with teachers on the brochure describing the intervention plans. They agreed to share draft copies, selected a protocol for receiving feedback, and committed to talking with students and parents before finalizing their brochures. Teacher teams worked together to read, research, and visit school sites that were successfully implementing a system of support. After several iterations, the district published three different brochures, one for each level, describing primary, elementary, and middle-level interventions and support.

The brochures were well received and represented a big improvement over existing practice; however, the action and support described were not perfect, and it wasn't long before they were revised. As teams implemented what they promised, they learned that some strategies worked better than others. New ideas quickly replaced the original ones, but they didn't view the changes as failures. Because the faculty had been engaged in *working* on the work, not reading about the work or talking about the work but actually *doing* the work from the start, there was a commitment to keep improving the intervention plans until schools got it right. The act of simply producing products had fostered the kind of action orientation that resulted in significant and lasting changes in practice.

This became a pattern and a way of working in the early days of PLC transformation in Kildeer District 96. The faculty and staff pushed through challenges with an action orientation. With hard work and persistence, in addition to the mindset of "progress over perfection" (T. Many, personal communication, December 3, 2018). District 96 became known as one of the highest achieving, lowest spending districts in the area, a model PLC school district, and became highly regarded for their work with all students, including those receiving special education services.

Doing Action Research

One of the ways an action orientation manifests itself in a PLC is through the process of action research. In the *Action Research Guidebook: A Process for Pursuing Equity and Excellence in Education*, Richard Sagor and Charlene Williams (2017) describe action research as "any investigation conducted by the person or the people empowered to take action concerning their own actions, for the purpose of improving their future actions" (p. 6). Action research is a process for engaging in the collaborative study of teaching and learning.

Sagor (2000) defines action research as "a disciplined process of inquiry conducted by and for those taking action" (p. 1). In education, individual teachers, collaborative teams, schools, and districts can conduct action research. More and more, teams are engaging in action research as a form of continuous improvement. Grade-level or departmental teams might use it as a process to explore intervention strategies for their students; school teams may form a taskforce to study homework policies and practices; and a district team may use a form of action research to engage in a review of its policies, practices, and procedures related to grading. As Sagor (2000) explains:

> Although we all know that research for its own sake is a worthy pursuit, the only justification for practicing K–12 educators to invest their finite time in research is if their particular inquiry holds promise for increasing the success of their teaching or the learning in their schools. (p. 7)

Understanding the Action Research Process

The focus of the action research, whatever problem or question the team decides to investigate, should be meaningful for those involved. Sagor and Williams (2017) argue that those in coaching roles must help teams answer three specific questions:

> 1) Is the focus on your professional action? 2) Are you empowered to adjust future action based on results? and 3) Is improvement possible? If the answer to these three questions is "yes," the team may want to employ action research as their strategy. (p. 7)

Throughout the process, teachers will ask, "What specifically did I do (the action)?; What improvement (the change) occurred for my students?; and What was the relationship between my actions and changes in performance?" (Sagor & Williams, 2017, p. 92). Most action research models have similar steps with minor variations including defining a problem and creating a vision, learning, devising a plan, acting, observing and collecting data, reflecting, and sharing.

Coaching is a highly effective way to provide job-embedded professional development within the context of the classroom. K. A. East (2015) points out that "PLCs offer a protected environment that encourages action and experimentation in pursuit of improved student learning" (p. 21). Developing the capacity of teachers to use action research to improve teaching and learning is a worthwhile goal for those coaching collaborative teams. Questions coaches can use to at each step of the action research process are as follows.

Step 1: Identify the Problem and Create a Vision

At this initial stage, coaches should ask the following questions: What problem are you addressing? Why is it important? What is your vision and what are some of the indicators for success? What is your theory of action? What do you expect to see at each stage and as an end result?

Step 2: Learn, Research, and Explore the Literature

Help teams formulate a plan by engaging in possibility thinking with the team. Questions that are appropriate for this stage include, What are other classrooms and schools doing to address the problem? Describe what they have done and the success they have had. Are there colleagues that you could partner with to research and learn? When will you visit or schedule a conversation to learn?

Step 3: Develop and Implement an Action Plan

Teams need to do the work, but coaching can support teams by facilitating the development and implementation of a plan. Questions coaches could consider at this point might be, What is your theory of action? What specific strategies will you employ? What group of students will you work with? What is the timeline?

Step 4: Observe and Collect Data

Coaches can model and play an important role by monitoring the collection of data. Ask probing questions like, What data will you collect? How will you collect it? What will you bring back to share in the next team meeting? What kind of process or which protocol will assist the team in discussing the data?

Step 5: Reflect and Share Results

In this last stage, coaching will encourage reflection on the results. Coaches may inquire by asking, What format and protocol will you use to share the data? How will the team respond to feedback and learning? What changes will you make now or in the future based on our results?

Applying Findings

Another positive outcome of action research conducted at the classroom level is that any findings are more likely to be accepted by practitioners. Thomas Guskey (2000a) explains why action research at the team level is so effective.

> The idea of action research is that educational problems and issues are best identified and investigated where the action is: at the classroom or school level. By integrating research into these settings and engaging those who work at this level in research activities, findings can be applied immediately, and problems solved more quickly. (p. 46)

Consider the following example from Mapleton Public Schools in Thornton, Colorado.

In the spring of 2018, Charlotte Ciancio, superintendent of schools in Mapleton Public Schools, mandated that effective June 1, 2018, the credit recovery program for high school students would be discontinued. The superintendent asked school and district leaders to form a district-level credit recovery task force to study the situation and develop recommendations (Toussaint, 2018).

The data suggested that too many students were involved in credit recovery, results were not acceptable, and many students used the program as their primary means of earning high school credit. According to one district-level director, the students took advantage of the fact that they could earn credits to pass even if they failed courses (Toussaint, 2018). The task force had three months to research viable alternatives to credit recovery and provide a report with specific recommendations for resolving the problem.

Rather than organizing a traditional taskforce, each high school in the district sent representatives to bimonthly meetings designed to provide the time and support necessary to engage in action research. Teams were guided through the process of (1) identifying the problem and creating the vision, (2) learning, researching, and exploring the literature, (3) developing and implementing an action plan, (4) observing and collecting data, and (5) reflecting and sharing any insights or results. The following list describes each step the task force took in more detail.

1. **Identifying the problem and creating the vision:** Teams began by analyzing current data, creating a vision for the desired outcome, and writing a problem of practice for the action research project.
2. **Learning, researching, and exploring the literature:** The team worked to clarify the contributing factors to lack of student success and began researching successful practices being implemented in other classrooms, schools, and districts experiencing similar challenges. They participated in literature reviews, collaborated with colleagues, and developed new ideas for solving the problem. Teams quickly realized that "credit recovery" was one strategy for helping struggling students. They would need to research why students were struggling and move to a system of support—not one strategy or program. Teams began simultaneously building relationships across the district, opening communication, and increasing transparency between the high schools.
3. **Developing and implementing an action plan:** Once teams identified the problem and reached consensus on the current reality of the situation, they quickly identified an action plan with the who, what, where, when, why, and how a team, or select group of teachers, would implement the vision and practices they identified. Teams and individual teachers worked to implement the action plan and test new strategies with students.
4. **Observing and collecting data:** By observing and collecting data throughout implementation of the action plan, teams found the need to make adjustments in details such as timelines for progress monitoring and developing commitment from participants.
5. **Reflecting and sharing insights and results:** During each large-group session, teams had time set aside to reflect, revise, and share results with colleagues from other schools. Teams used inquiry processes and protocols to aid in their self-reflection.

Some of the focus areas included grading policies and procedures, formative assessment practices with demonstration of learning, and reading progression and comprehension. Some of the feedback from early on in the project included observations from leaders highlighting shifts in teachers' assessment practices, a higher quarter pass rate, and greater ownership of their own learning by students. Participants also reported improvement in reading and comprehension and the implementation of student support structures during the advisory period. One anonymous evaluation collected at the end of a taskforce session in May 2018 stated the following:

> The structure of this process was extremely effective. Isolate the challenge, research the issue, carry out action research, and PUT A PLAN INTO ACTION. It was amazing to be open and collaborative with all high schools in the district.

The knowledge and new learning associated with this action research project generated some very promising results, such as increased collaboration and improved processes for exploring issues and taking action. The experience of participating in this action research helped teams embrace continuous improvement as a way of working and contributed to creating more momentum around learning in the schools.

Ultimately, the task force changed its name to the intervention task force and refocused the team's purpose from credit recovery to helping students meet academic outcomes by providing additional time and support through a schoolwide system of intervention. We believe that the action research process contributed to more focused supports for students in the participating high schools, and the expectation that credit recovery will eventually become past practice.

In the following section, we explore how coaching action research routines and habits are more effective when teams use the action research SIG as their reference point and the pathways tool to monitor next steps.

Using the Action-Orientation SIG and Pathways Tools

The action orientation SIG in figure 5.1, with its anchor statement, indicators, and descriptors, provides a flight plan that is beneficial in helping coaches and teams understand their current state of action orientation as well as determine next possible best steps for a team. Connecting feedback and support to the tool will help propel teams forward to a stronger action orientation.

<table>
<tr><th colspan="3">Anchor Statement</th></tr>
<tr><td colspan="3">Teams have a sense of urgency in approaching their work and use inquiry and continuous improvement processes as they collaborate. They are action oriented and relentless about improving teaching and learning for students.</td></tr>
<tr><th>Beyond Proficient</th><th>Proficient</th><th>Below Proficient</th></tr>
<tr><td>Teams believe in the critical role they play in a student's life. They seek knowledge and use data and research to act quickly to support learning.
Teams are results oriented and have limited SMART goals connected to school and district goals. They set short-term goals and monitor results on a continuous basis. They set benchmarks to measure progress.
Teams are persistent and tenacious in pursuit of student learning. When they are faced with an obstacle, they put plans and actions in place quickly. They pre-empt many challenges by predicting and anticipating conditions and factors.
Teams frequently create common products to stay focused on the learning target or the outcome they are seeking. They review and seek improvement in the products on a continual basis.
Teams use continuous improvement processes, such as action research and lesson study, to address challenges and improvements in teaching and learning.
Teams design and take responsibility for their own professional learning connected to student needs. They identify knowledge, skills, and practices to improve upon and create learning opportunities while on the job. They evaluate the new learning and relationship to student progress.
Teams' actions are growth oriented. They are not afraid to take risks and fail. They are transparent and seek assistance from one another. Teams become more curious and creative in their work as they test new ideas.</td><td>Teams believe in the critical role they play in a student's life and act now (not later) to support their learning
Teams are results oriented with limited short-term SMART goals.
Teams monitor achievement of the goals using benchmarks.
Teams are persistent and tenacious in their pursuit of student learning. When they are faced with an obstacle, they create plans to address it.
Teams frequently create common products to stay focused on the learning target or the outcome they are seeking.
Teams use continuous improvement processes such as action research to address challenges in teaching and learning.
Teams design and take responsibility for their own professional learning connected to student needs. They identify knowledge, skills, and practices to improve upon and create learning opportunities while on the job.
Teams' actions are growth oriented. They are not afraid to take risks and fail. They are transparent and seek assistance from one another.</td><td>Teams believe in the critical role they play in a student's life. They identify strategies to support their learning.
Teams develop specific goals to guide their work in teams.
Teams are persistent in pursuit of student learning and identify factors that may be obstacles.
Teams create common products occasionally.
Teams use a variety of processes to overcome challenges in teaching and learning.
Teams participate in professional learning connected to student needs.
Teams commit to be growth oriented and identify norms that will remind them that failure is part of learning.</td></tr>
</table>

Figure 5.1: Action orientation SIG.

Visit ***go.SolutionTree.com/PLCbooks*** *for a free reproducible version of this figure.*

A coach can also support teams by using the pathways tool for action orientation (figure 5.2). The tool incorporates a series of hierarchical questions that help both the coach and the team understand where the next level of support might take place. In addition to planning, the questions are appropriate for faculties and teacher teams as starters for focused conversations. The coach could also use the tool in an activity with a product orientation. In a professional learning session, table teams may answer the questions on charts and share with colleagues. Similarities and differences in thinking will be transparent and lead to more meaningful dialogue and understanding.

Act to Make a Difference in Student Learning	**Use SMART Goals to Measure Success**	**Address Obstacles in a Persistent Manner**	**Create Common Products**
What will occur for our students if we do not act? What evidence do we need before we would act? What do we need to know before we will act?	What do we expect to see when students meet proficiency? What do we expect to see as students work towards proficiency? What kind of system will help in tracking and monitoring goals for the teacher, team, and students?	Do we expect any challenges or obstacles? What strategies will pre-empt or deter the challenges? What norms will help us stay resourceful in challenging times?	What are the expectations related to common products? What are the expectations for the frequency of creating common products?

Action Research Process	**Participation in Ongoing Professional Development**	**Maintain a Growth Mindset Encourage Taking Risks**
What model may move our team(s) to action? How does it connect to the work in the collaborative team? What are the benefits and outcomes related to a model we are considering using? What is the timeline for implementation?	How will the team pursue professional learning? What are the expectations related to job-embedded learning? What tool or model of professional learning best connects with the defined goals?	What is our philosophy and reaction to failing? How do we communicate our results? How do we support one another? How do we use our norms to address transparency, failing and growing? How comfortable are we with trying new ways of doing things and taking risks?

Figure 5.2: Pathways for an action orientation.

*Visit **go.SolutionTree.com/PLCbooks** for a free reproducible version of this figure.*

Moving Forward

In *Learning by Doing*, DuFour et al. (2016) express their greatest hope that their work will:

> Help educators take immediate and specific steps to close the knowing-doing gap in education by implementing the PLC process . . . to eliminate excuses for inaction and convince educators that the best way to become more effective in the PLC process is to begin doing what PLCs do. (p. 19)

Teachers in a PLC act with a sense of urgency. In the next chapter, we explore how teams translate an action orientation into the real, tangible outcomes they seek by focusing on results.

Summary

- Teams improve and are more motivated when they learn by doing.
- Teams in a PLC act with a sense of urgency; they act with a resolve and level of determination that places student learning as the team's highest priority.
- Action orientation is about diagnosing, planning, engaging in the work, reflecting, and making adjustments.
- What distinguishes an action orientation in a PLC is that team actions are not arbitrary or random; they are deliberate and purposeful.
- Action-oriented teams create products and explicit strategies and use them in teaching and learning.
- Action research is a process with defined steps for acquiring new knowledge and insights and applying it to future actions.
- Developing the capacity of teachers to use action research to improve teaching and learning is a worthwhile goal for those coaching collaborative teams.

Reflection Questions

A coach plays an instrumental role in cultivating the conditions that are necessary for an action orientation to thrive. As you reflect on the content of this chapter, consider the following two questions.

1. Is your team purposeful in its actions? Describe the concrete tools, products, and strategies your team uses to improve teaching and learning through action orientation.
2. Is your team struggling or facing an obstacle in its work? Define an area of concern and your vision for your desired state. What are the benefits and what would it take for your team to engage in an action research process?

CHAPTER 6

Getting Better—The Significance of a Results Orientation

Change is the end result of all true learning.

—LEO BUSCAGLIA

In prior chapters, we discussed the essential elements of collective inquiry, continuous improvement, and action orientation. We are discussing results orientation last because, in the end, all the other essential elements lead to results.

Since the implementation of No Child Left Behind in 2001, the landscape of public education has become increasingly results oriented. We see examples of this with teacher evaluation programs, state school rankings, and letter grades assigned to both whole districts and individual schools. Although these results often carry negative connotations, a results orientation *can* be a positive thing!

PLCs pride themselves on maintaining a focus on learning, one of the three big ideas of a PLC (DuFour et al., 2016). When teams are focused on learning, they not only use results to identify students who need additional time and support, but they also use results to identify gaps or concerns in curriculum and instructional practice. What may be most important is that team members use results to push themselves to improve their instructional practices that result in increased student achievement.

Not so long ago it was the norm for teachers to identify a successful lesson by determining whether or not students liked it. Teachers had good intentions and designed lessons they felt would adequately cover the material and hold the students' interest. In this case, the criteria for success was based on feelings rather than results. We can have great intentions and feel like we are making progress, but until we can *see* the difference in results, we are spinning our wheels. According to Hattie (2009), "The education profession will not mature as a profession until professional dialogue focuses on evidence of student learning rather than opinions" (p. 259). Results-oriented teams crave evidence that shows whether their efforts are producing the outcomes they intended. Results provide us with guidance on what we are doing well and where we need to make adjustments.

To be successful, a for-profit business must be focused on results. If a bakery does not sell a specific number of sweet treats, it will not make enough money to pay its employees, rent the facility, or buy ingredients for the next day's doughnuts. So the owner calculates how many baked goods he must sell in order to turn a profit, and he and his staff set a sales goal for each day. The team uses past sales records to determine which baked goods sell fastest and have the highest profit margin, and they respond accordingly by baking more of those products. At the end of each day, the manager reviews the sales to determine whether they met their goal. The manager uses those results to make adjustments to the plan.

As educators, our product is student learning. It is our job to identify what our students need to know and be able to do, set goals for achievement levels, and deliver instruction using effective instructional strategies. Like the baker, we monitor our results and make adjustments to the plan in order to ensure all students are learning at high levels.

Maintaining a results orientation also contributes to a positive staff culture. According to Value Based Management (2016), people will work with more enthusiasm and have more fun if they:

- Clearly know what is expected of them;
- Are involved in establishing these expectations;
- Are allowed to determine for themselves how they are going to meet these expectations; and
- Obtain feedback about their performance

Although these ideas are based on a business model, they relate directly to schools and, specifically, to collaborative teams working in a PLC. Teachers working as part of a PLC will accomplish more when they know what they are working toward, have a hand in creating the expectations, are allowed a certain amount of autonomy in determining methods for reaching the goals, and are provided with ongoing, high-leverage feedback about their progress.

Authors at Value Based Management (2016) describe the process of becoming results oriented in business with the following steps:

- Setting long-term corporate goals
- Translating corporate goals to divisional and individual goals

- Making results-oriented agreements about goals
- Implementing, self-steering, and reporting (management)
- Making periodic appraisals, controlling progress, and making adjustments

We argue that similar steps are necessary for teams to become results oriented in a PLC (see table 6.1).

Table 6.1: The Process of Becoming Results Oriented

Business Setting	Collaborative Teams in a PLC
Setting long-term corporate goals	Setting schoolwide goals
Translating corporate goals to divisional and individual goals	Translating school goals to content-area or grade- level collaborative team goals
Making results-oriented agreements about goals	Making results-oriented agreements about goals, and making goals SMART
Implementing, self-steering, and reporting (management)	Making team decisions about instructional strategies to reach the goals, for implementation, self-steering, and team reporting
Making periodic appraisals, controlling progress, and making adjustments	Monitoring and adjusting by teams through common formative and summative assessments Monitoring progress with conversations between the principal or coach and teams

Collaborative teams in a PLC develop their own SMART goals that are aligned with school and district goals. They are trusted to conduct research (action orientation) on best practice instructional strategies and implement the methods that will best help them accomplish these goals. In so doing, teams develop a sense of ownership and commitment to reaching these collective goals. Simultaneously, team members begin to hold one another mutually accountable as they develop their own collaborative culture while principals and coaches engage in regular, ongoing progress monitoring processes with the teams.

Creating a Results-Oriented Culture

When we relentlessly pursue our mission and vision of high levels of learning for *all students*, we are hyper-focused on results, what they mean, and how they can help us improve. Principals and coaches can begin making a results orientation part of the school culture by focusing on data themselves. Principals and coaches who present relevant data and model its use to improve student achievement are building a culture where results are valued rather than feared. The school's leadership team acts as a model for how grade-level or content-area teams should operate by setting school SMART goals, using formative data to measure progress and determine next steps, and celebrating when teams meet goals. When administrators and coaches lead by example and provide clear expectations for how teams should use results, they begin to create a culture of results orientation.

Although modeling the use of data is a powerful strategy, it is often not enough. Coaches and leaders must provide teams with direct instruction coupled with hands-on experience on how to analyze common assessment data and how to use the results to improve learning. Systems for data-analysis protocols, storage, access, and sharing must all be put into place in order for results orientation to become an integral part of a school culture. One way to provide teams with clarity of expectations and procedures is to engage staff in the development of a SIG to help teams identify their current reality and plan their next steps in the development of a results orientation. (See the section Using the Results-Orientation SIG and Pathways Tools on page 89 for more on this strategy.)

By providing teams with a clear picture of the end goal, they are far more likely to reach it. When coaches use the SIG in combination with ongoing feedback and support, teams get even further, faster. According to Killion (2015), "It is the feedback process that leads to achieving results, especially when the feedback process is designed to develop knowledge, skills, and practices and motivation to act upon the feedback to generate results" (p. 18).

As part of their ongoing feedback and support, many successful PLC principals and coaches meet with collaborative teams on a regular basis to maintain a results orientation. These leaders engage teams in conversations about the essential standards they are teaching, the data that shows how students are progressing, the interventions teams are using, and reflections on instructional practices. These meetings allow the leader to keep a pulse on the achievement levels in their buildings. Paul Bambrick-Santoyo (2012) states the following:

> When these meetings succeed, they are the apex of a data cycle that shifts a school's focus to the most fundamental question of education: not "Did we teach it?" but "Did the students learn it? And, if they didn't, how can we teach it so that they do?" (p. 23)

In other words, maintaining a results orientation helps keep schools focused on learning, one of the three big ideas of a PLC (DuFour et al., 2016).

Measuring Progress

It is a general expectation that teachers monitor their students' progress throughout the school year, providing students and parents with frequent updates about successes, challenges, and next steps for learning. Regularly scheduled data meetings between school leaders and their collaborative teams also allow principals and coaches to monitor the successes, challenges, and next steps for learning of their collaborative teams. These conversations can reveal elements of the relationship among team members, how teams are spending their time, and the degree to which team members feel comfortable reflecting upon their own instructional practices. Leaders can use these indicators to determine the type of coaching and support each team needs to continue their growth toward the SIG's gold standards. While some teams may need very directive feedback about next steps for growth, other teams may simply need to review their short-term goals and celebrate small wins to keep the positive momentum going. In both cases, meeting regularly to monitor the progress of each collaborative team is an essential component to maintaining a results orientation in a PLC.

Likewise, in many successful districts, central office administrators meet regularly with building principals and coaches to obtain a pulse on each building in the district. This cycle of vertical and horizontal accountability fosters a results orientation wherein all members of the instructional leadership team are expected to have an intimate knowledge of the instructional happenings within their sphere of influence.

While face-to-face meetings are an important part of maintaining a results orientation, there are a myriad of mechanisms leaders can use to measure a team's progress and provide them with ongoing feedback and support. Principals, coaches and other leaders who have access to teams' written products or artifacts such as meeting minutes have a tremendous opportunity to formatively assess their teams' progress toward a results orientation. These documents can reveal whether teams respond to the four critical questions, how often they discuss specific topics, the types of interventions they plan for struggling students and, of course, their assessment results data. Just as good teachers use formative data to provide their students with feedback about their progress toward proficiency, leaders can use the information they learn from team artifacts to provide teams with feedback about their progress, celebrate short term wins, and stress the expectations for a results orientation.

We have seen several other creative ways of maintaining a results orientation in a PLC. One Macomb County, Michigan, principal asks her teams to present to the rest of the staff at the end of each instructional unit. The team tells its story, including the unit SMART goal, successful strategies they used, and the interventions and extensions they provided. They share the challenges they encountered and their methods for overcoming them. Best of all, they celebrate their results together, not only as a team, but as an entire faculty working together to achieve high levels of learning for all students. Another principal we know engages in collaborative team meeting walkthroughs. Each week he observes a different team meeting, using the PLC SIG to identify the team's current reality and determine where they might be ready to move to next. Please see *Amplify Your Impact* (Many et al., 2018) pages 59–60 for an example PLC SIG. He uses the Pathways for the Four Critical Questions of Learning (see *Amplify Your Impact* [Many et al., 2018]) to guide his questioning and feedback. And in a third district, the superintendent meets with his principals monthly for performance-management meetings. These discussions center around a common set of data that all buildings are expected to collect such as student attendance, discipline, teacher attendance, student mobility, use of high-quality instructional strategies, and achievement results on common assessments. The superintendent and principal discuss the data, plans for improvement, and support the principal needs from central office to make those improvements. In this case, each school building is constantly focused on the results and making plans for incremental improvements, using PLC as the heart of the school improvement process.

All of these examples demonstrate an expectation that results are valued and utilized to determine next steps and celebrate successes. No matter what method they use, it is imperative that leaders and coaches make expectations for a results orientation clear. As teams dive into the expectations of a results-oriented culture, they begin monitoring themselves for effectiveness rather than waiting for the formal monitoring mechanisms we described here. The Pathways for a Results Orientation (see the section Using the Results-Orientation SIG and Pathways Tools for more on this strategy) identifies the tasks that teams will turn into routines and, eventually, into habits of practice.

Broadening the Definition of Results

When building PLCs, collaborative team members put themselves in a vulnerable position. PLCs strive to build a culture where team members trust each other enough to share achievement results that can be directly attributed to their instruction. But the ultimate results PLCs seek go far beyond a test score a student may achieve on any particular day. A results orientation should ultimately be focused on changing teachers' instructional practice.

The hope is that teachers will reflect not only on assessment data but also on the ways their instructional decisions, routines, and habits of professional practice impacted that data. In other words, teachers should connect student results to their own teaching. They should ask themselves not just, "Did my students learn it?" but also, "How effective was my instruction? What could I have done differently that would have yielded better results?" Arriving at a place where teachers can ask themselves those questions (and answer them honestly) takes a certain amount of trust, maturity, and self-confidence. Most collaborative teams must go through an evolutionary cycle in order to reach this level of self-reflection. It is the coaches' job to nudge teams along in this evolutionary cycle. Teams that reach these levels of self-reflection and take the opportunity to change their practice based on student assessment results have produced the ultimate desired result: improved instructional habits of practice that lead to increased student achievement. Figure 1.6 shows the steps teams take to build a results orientation.

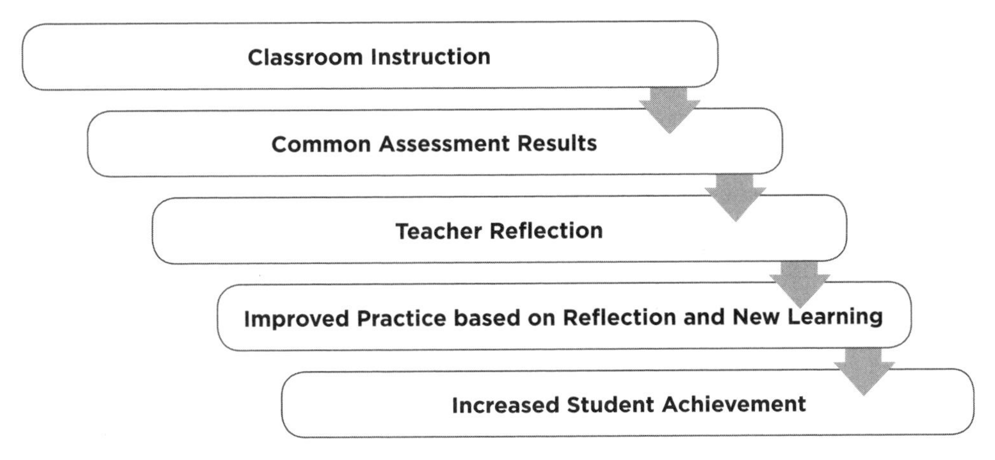

Figure 6.1: Team steps toward results orientation.

Using the Results-Orientation SIG and Pathways Tools

The results-orientation SIG in figure 6.2, with its anchor statement, indicators, and descriptors, provides a flight plan that is beneficial in helping coaches and teams understand their current state of results-orientation as well as determine next possible best steps for a team. Connecting feedback and support to the tool will help propel teams forward to a stronger results-orientation.

Anchor Statement		
Efforts are measured by results rather than intentions. All initiatives are subjected to ongoing assessment on the basis of tangible results.		
Beyond Proficient	**Proficient**	**Below Proficient**
Team members collaboratively develop short-and long-term SMART goals based on student achievement and teacher effectiveness data.	Team members collaboratively develop short- and long-term SMART goals and regularly monitor their progress toward these goals.	Team members collaboratively develop SMART goals and monitor their progress toward the goals.

Figure 6.2: Results-orientation SIG.

continued →

Beyond Proficient	Proficient	Below Proficient
Teams have a planned method and schedule for monitoring their progress toward these goals. Teams collaboratively develop valid and reliable common formative and summative assessments to measure students' attainment of essential standards and learning targets. Teams collaboratively analyze assessment results to identify student needs and plan student interventions at the learning target level. Teams collaboratively analyze data to reflect on program effectiveness and make revisions based on the data. Teams collaboratively analyze data to reflect on individual and team instructional practices and make improvements based on the data. Teams celebrate reaching short-term and long-term SMART goals and identify ways to replicate positive results.	Teams collaboratively develop common formative and summative assessments to measure students' attainment of essential standards. Teams collaboratively analyze assessment results to identify student needs and plan student interventions. Teams collaboratively analyze assessment results to reflect on program effectiveness and individual and team instructional practices. Teams celebrate reaching short-term SMART goals.	Teams collaboratively develop common summative assessments to measure students' attainment of essential standards. Teams collaboratively analyze assessment results to make decisions for instructional next steps. Teams collaboratively analyze assessment results to identify problems in program effectiveness.

Visit ***go.SolutionTree.com/PLCbooks*** *for a free reproducible version of this figure.*

A coach can also support teams by using the pathways tool for a results orientation (figure 6.3). The tool incorporates a series of hierarchical questions that help both the coach and the team understand where the next level of support might take place. Consider this tool a catalyst or a springboard to the coaching process. For example, a principal acting as a coach can take the pathways tool with her when she attends a collaborative team meeting, identifying which pathway the team is addressing. As the team members engage in their conversation, the principal (coach) can use the pathway questions to guide the team's comments, statements, and questions. In other cases, a coach can direct the pathways questions to the leadership team as a means of helping them shape policies and practices that lead to a results-oriented culture.

Developing SMART Goals	Planning for SMART Goal Attainment	Developing Common Assessments	Analyzing Common Assessment Data	Sharing Assessment Results
What professional learning do staff members need on why SMART goals are important and how to write them? What are the expectations for frequency and duration of team short-term SMART goals? What are the expectations for the alignment of team-developed long-term SMART goals with building goals? How are building long-term SMART goals aligned with district goals? Who will collect and review SMART goals and how?	What protocols are in place for teams to plan toward attainment of SMART goals? When are teams provided time to collaboratively research, identify, and plan the use of best practice strategies that will lead them to the attainment of SMART goals? How do teams utilize data from previously used strategies to make decisions about future instruction? Who collects and reviews plans for SMART goal attainment and how? Who monitors plans for SMART goal attainment for progress and how?	What are the expectations for frequency of common formative assessments? What are the expectations for frequency of common summative assessments? To what degree do teams have the knowledge and skills needed to create valid and reliable common assessments? What professional development is available to assist teams in creating valid and reliable assessments? How do teams know on which standards they should base their common assessments? What processes and protocols exist to help teams use data to revise assessment items? What are the expectations for the timing and administration conditions of common assessments?	How do teams obtain timely access to common assessment data? To what level do teams have the knowledge and skills needed to analyze common assessment data? What professional development is available for teams who need additional support in analyzing assessment data? Who is responsible for facilitating common assessment data-analysis meetings? What district or building protocols exist to assist teams in analyzing assessment data? How are teams expected to respond to assessment data? What is the process for teams to record data analysis conclusions and plans for responding to the data? How are teams encouraged to utilize common assessment data to identify which students need additional time and support related to specific standards and targets? How are teams expected to support students struggling in specific standards or target areas? How are teams encouraged to utilize assessment data to reflect on the effectiveness of core instruction, reflect on individual and team instructional practices, and use the data to learn from their colleagues?	How often are teams expected to share common assessment results? With whom? What results are teams expected to share? In what format are teams expected to share their results? What information are teams expected to share in addition to data (such as intervention plans, extension activities, instructional strategies, reflection on effectiveness of instruction, and so on)? How will celebration be included in the sharing process?

Figure 6.3: Pathways for results orientation.

*Visit **go.SolutionTree.com/PLCbooks** for a free reproducible version of this figure.*

Moving Forward

Test scores are a means to an end, not the end itself. When collaborative team members utilize assessment results to reflect on and make improvements to their own teaching practices, educators are far more likely to achieve increased student achievement. According to Bambrick-Santoyo (2012), "Great leaders make sure that the results of data analysis meetings translate into real classroom changes. . . . Assessment is useless until it affects instruction" (p. 46). We have all seen cases where teams have reviewed assessment data and provided interventions, only to have the interventions use similar instructional practices as the original teaching, resulting in little to no improvement in student mastery. It is only when teachers and collaborative teams utilize assessment results to reflect on and change their own practices that teams truly develop a results orientation. Coaches can be instrumental in moving teams toward this level of self-reflection. By building team members' trust, clarifying expectations, asking thought-provoking questions, and celebrating small wins, coaches can help teachers move from reviewing numbers to improving instructional practice. In the following chapter, we discuss ways coaches can assess a team's current reality and help the team navigate through the developmental process of the essential elements of a PLC.

Summary

- Results-oriented teams crave evidence that show whether their efforts are producing the outcomes they intended. When they are not achieving the results they seek, these teams make adjustments to ensure all students are learning at high levels.
- Working toward common goals and celebrating when those goals are met strengthens collaborative teams and improves school culture.
- Coaches and leaders must provide teams with direct instruction on how to analyze common assessment data and how to use the results to improve teacher practices and student results. Systems for data-analysis protocols, storage, access, and sharing must all be put into place in order for results orientation to become an integral part of a school culture.
- Coaches and leaders must continually monitor the results-orientation levels of each team and provide them with ongoing feedback and support to build a results orientation. The goal is for teams to develop a habit of practice of monitoring their own results orientation themselves.

- The ultimate goal is for teachers to reflect on student results and make improvements to their own practice. It is these instructional improvements that will lead to increased student achievement.

Reflection Questions

A coach plays an instrumental role in cultivating the conditions that are necessary for a results orientation to thrive. As you reflect on the content of this chapter, consider the following four questions.

1. How are you monitoring the results-orientation levels of the teams in your building?
2. How do teams share their results outside of the team?
3. How are teachers held accountable for reflection and instructional improvements based on results?
4. How do you celebrate short-term wins in your building?

PART III

COACHING COLLABORATIVE TEAMS IN PLCs AT WORK

CHAPTER 7

Assessing a Team's Current Reality

When educators learn to clarify their priorities, to assess the current reality of their situation, to work together, and to build continuous improvement into the very fabric of their collective work, they create conditions for the ongoing learning and self-efficacy essential to solving whatever problems they confront.

—RICHARD DUFOUR, REBECCA DUFOUR, ROBERT EAKER, TOM MANY, AND MIKE MATTOS

In chapter 1, we argued that the goal of those who coach collaborative teams should be to help teams *get better at getting better*. If the mission of our schools is to ensure all students learn to high levels, those in coaching roles must help teams do the following three things: (1) clarify the mission-critical practices teachers should embrace; (2) provide teams with the right kind of feedback at the right time; and (3) support teams in their efforts to ensure high levels of learning for all.

Merriam-Webster (2019) defines competence as having sufficient knowledge, skill, or strength. As with any set of skills, there are varying levels of competence, and the process of becoming a high-performing collaborative team is no different. Becoming a high-performing collaborative team is a process that takes time and patience—and we would argue coaching—to become truly competent in all of the different aspects of the PLC process. In this chapter, we provide coaches with a guide to help ascertain how competent the teams they are working with are in each of the essential elements of a PLC.

Since implementing the PLC process is not a cookie-cutter approach, one cannot determine a timeline to move between stages of competence. So often, we have heard that leaders would like to know when their teams would "get it" and become high functioning. Educators historically operated from a beginning-to-end of year timeline mentality, but implementing the PLC process is contrary to this mindset.

Becoming a PLC is an enigmatic process due to the variables in individuals' skill sets, propensity toward professional change, and factors leading to strong collaboration.

In the 1970s, Noel Burch, an employee at Gordon Training International, developed a theory called the Four Stages of Competence (Gordon & Burch, 1977; figure 7.1).

1. Unconscious incompetence
2. Conscious incompetence
3. Conscious competence
4. Unconscious competence

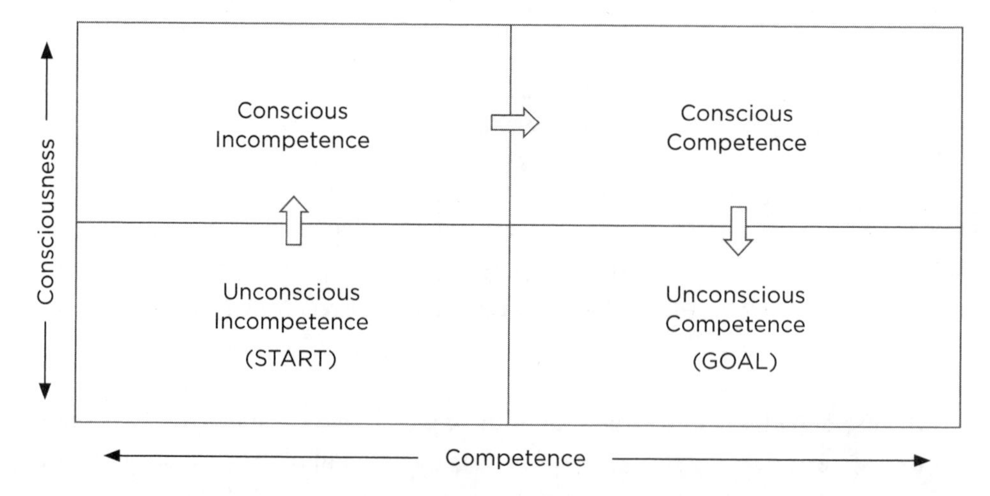

Source: Gordon & Burch, 1977, pp. 4-14, 4-15. Reprinted with permission from www.gordontraining.com.

Figure 7.1: The Four Stages of Competence.

We share his thinking in relation to PLC implementation as it parallels the process teachers undergo as they become a high-functioning collaborative team within a PLC.

Using the Four Stages of Competence

PLC transformation is a process teams become more competent in over time. Teachers begin implementing the PLC process at the unconsciously incompetent stage and move clockwise to the unconsciously competent stage (see figure 7.1). In the following sections, we examine how those in coaching roles respond to the general needs of teams in each stage of the model. Beyond this, we explore the specific coaching elements teams will need for each of the four essential elements at each stage of learning.

Although the text is laid out in a linear fashion, this chapter is designed so that a coach, principal, or other leader can go directly to the essential element on which a team is working, identify the stage of learning, and glean specific information on how to help move the team forward in that essential element. Our hope is that readers will use this chapter on an as-needed basis to support their coaching practices, specific to the needs of individual teams. In addition, we have provided a support document, in appendix A (page 127), that summarizes this information.

Coaching Unconsciously Incompetent Teams

In this stage, teams don't know what they don't know. Teachers may have heard of PLCs from colleagues in other districts or attended a one-day overview of the PLC process, but most don't really know what it takes to successfully implement the PLC process. Teachers often from the same team or department—make completely contradictory statements like, "I know what PLCs are" or "I have never heard of PLCs." Others ask, "What does PLC stand for?" only to have their colleagues dismiss their question with comments like "We did PLCs ten years ago!" This stage is a common starting place, and, without the proper coaching, teams flounder as teachers are left to sort fact from fiction.

When working with teams in the unconsciously incompetent stage, the coach's primary goal is to build shared knowledge of the PLC process. Coaches focus on creating clarity by providing teams with lots of information; articles, workshops, and visitations are all terrific sources of information about the PLC process. By design, feedback from the coach is direct and any support is concrete and specific. Team goals are purposefully attainable and designed to promote the celebration of small wins.

Early in a school's PLC journey is the time to engage teachers in conversations about their beliefs. Coaches can provide teachers with opportunities to reflect on how their beliefs align with the notion that all kids can learn. This is also when coaches help teams commit to learning as the fundamental purpose of their school and begin to generate collective agreement among and between teachers as to why the PLC process is important.

It is not unusual for teachers in this stage to have lots of misinterpretations or misunderstandings about the PLC process. Coaches can minimize ambiguity by creating a common vocabulary that teams use to sort through their misconceptions with a minimum of confusion; those in coaching roles often shift the traditional use of time in faculty meetings for just this purpose. Rather than reviewing a litany of procedural issues, coaches use the time to clarify the meaning of important PLC terminology. Comparing and contrasting the meaning of terms such as *collaboration* and *cooperation*, *intervention* and *remediation*, or *formative* and *summative* is a worthwhile use of time. Plus, doing this kind of work accomplishes two things: it helps build shared knowledge and reinforces the message that school leaders value the PLC process.

In this stage, teachers are not yet able to identify the mission-critical behaviors present on highly effective teams because they haven't had enough experience with the PLC process to know what is important. Consequently, teams have not established any routines, nor have they developed any habits around their professional practice.

Patience is important at this stage; one of the most common mistakes those in coaching roles make is to be too ambitious thereby creating unreasonable expectations around the work. Some of the most effective leaders declare the first year of their PLC initiative as "a year of learning," which allows everyone to concentrate on building shared knowledge of the PLC process. For teams in the unconsciously incompetent stage, coaches and principals should understand that simply establishing meaningful teams, creating norms, setting SMART goals, developing common vocabulary, and building a shared knowledge about what a PLC is and is not can be quite an accomplishment!

Coaching Consciously Incompetent Teams

Teams in the consciously incompetent stage know what they don't know and recognize their vulnerabilities. Teachers on these teams say things like, "We have a long way to go" or "This was helpful, but I'm not sure working in teams is going to last." Others may comment (with a deep sigh), "Getting everyone onboard is a challenge. I'm willing to try; I just hope my teammates are too," or "This sure took a long time; I hope the results are worth it."

The foremost challenge when working with consciously incompetent teams is to identify and describe specific behaviors that are critical to the success of collaborative teams. Even though these teams can name the different elements of the PLC process, every task is deliberate and time consuming. The PLC process feels methodical, even somewhat awkward to teams and coaches must remind teachers that what takes forever now will become more expeditious as their PLC practice become more routinized and habitual.

Teams operating in the consciously incompetent stage have enough background knowledge and experience with the PLC process to identify the mission-critical practices that are present on highly effective teams but have not yet established routines, and thus have not developed any habits around their professional practice. Coaches continue to provide information and promote clarity by asking teams to decide what they must stop, start, and keep doing to become highly effective. A coach's feedback moves back and forth between the direct and conversational stances and support is designed to move teams toward consensus around which tasks are critical to accomplishing the school's mission of learning for all.

At this stage, teaming is a fragile concept. Collaboration is a big shift from isolation, and remains a new experience for most teachers who, by now, have seen the novelty of working in teams wear off. It is important that those in coaching roles strike a balance between encouragement and expectations because without effective coaching, teams will quickly revert to past practice.

Coaching Consciously Competent Teams

Teams functioning in the consciously competent stage know what they know and engage in the work of fully implementing the PLC process. Collaborative teams meet on a regular basis and teachers are aware that student growth is directly tied to their work. One might hear, "Our PLCs are truly making a difference for students!" and "At our school, collaboration is the way we plan and implement lessons. We love working together on behalf of our students!"

The most productive role for coaches working with consciously competent teams is to focus on the development of routines. In stage 2 (consciously incompetent), teams identified the individual tasks associated with the PLC process, in stage 3 (consciously competent), the team's productivity grows as individual tasks are combined into routines. Coaches encourage teams to repeat the routines on a regular basis and although a few routines start to become habits, teams are not conscious about scaffolding multiple routines into habits. Teachers have also not begun the process of systematically stacking individual habits into larger and more complex habits of professional practice.

At this stage, coaches will find that clarity is really about reinforcing, refining, and occasionally reframing the knowledge teams have acquired during implementation. The most common feedback stance combines collaborative and reflective questions and coaching support takes the form of using the pathways tools to guide teams toward deeper levels of understanding around their PLC practice. In this stage, coaches and leaders may feel that teams are well on their way to becoming interdependent and high-functioning, but it is best to continue engaging teams and monitoring their progress.

Coaching Unconsciously Competent Teams

The final stage in Burch's model (Adams, n.d.) is unconsciously competent. Teachers can be heard saying things like, "This make so much sense," and "Why did it take so long for us to see the value of PLCs?" or "We don't do PLCs; we are a PLC!" Unconsciously competent teams truly own the PLC process.

At this stage, the faculty know what to do and have incorporated the PLC process into the culture of their teams. These teachers have acquired a deep understanding of the PLC process and the coach's role is to promote self-reflection and discovery by the team. These teams regularly engage in action research and often coach each other toward higher and higher levels of sophistication around the PLC process. Feedback is primarily aimed at encouraging teams to drill deeper; support is designed to encourage teams to examine topics that are typically not undertaken by teams.

Teams at the unconsciously competent stage naturally meet, plan, and implement the PLC process as a whole unit. Instead of going through an orientation process with principals or coaches, new staff members are assimilated, and colleagues teach them the PLC processes. These teams have identified the tasks and developed routines that they have practiced until they become habits that are then stacked one atop the next to create comprehensive habits of professional practice.

Coaching the Essential Elements as Teams Move Through the Quadrants

As we described earlier, teams will need differentiated coaching according to their specific needs. While every team has a unique identity and coaching is most effective when tailored to the unique needs of each team, there are strategies coaches can use as teams cycle through each of Burch's stages of learning. In the following paragraphs, we illustrate how coaches work with teams on each of the essential elements of the PLC process.

Moving Through the Quadrants for Collective Inquiry

Teams operating at the unconscious incompetence stage are easily identifiable. The individual teachers rarely function as a team, often resist working together or with a coach, and rely on past practice reflected in instructional strategies that may or may not provide positive results for students. The team tends to cherry pick student successes while rationalizing or attributing failure to the lack of student engagement or prerequisite skills. These teams make decisions regarding student learning based on individual preferences, perceptions, and opinion with limited or no inquiry or collaboration.

In this stage, the coach is hands on, taking an active role to model and provide consultant-level feedback to raise awareness. Teams explore the SIG to heighten understanding about collective inquiry and associated tasks and routines. The coach plays a very active role and also must be prepared to respond to resistant behavior from team members.

At a consciously incompetent stage, teams realize that collaboration could benefit their students however, working together, as a team, isn't natural, often needing to be scheduled and closely monitored. Teams use data in a limited way during conversations and decision making. As a team, there is compliance and conversations that challenge another colleague's point of view are rare. Trust among team members is low, and there isn't a propensity to be vulnerable. As the team collaborates and small wins occur, they begin to recognize that they can influence student learning.

The consciously incompetent stage is where coaches begin to feel hopeful that change will occur. Coaches continue to play an integral role with continued modeling, guiding, and providing resources. The team continually references the SIG and uses the pathways for inquiry, but most of the time the coach still leads the work.

Teams that identify as consciously competent function at a high level yet recognize that their practice is an ever-changing and evolving process. These teams use data to determine instructional success and view the collective intelligence of the team as the primary source of solutions for their students. The team demonstrates respect, trust, and support for one another through their actions and language, and when these teams disagree or cannot reach a consensus, they are able to withstand conflict because their pattern of questioning allows for cognitive dissonance about the ideas at hand. They persevere and work to reach consensus on a solution that accommodates everyone's view.

At this stage, coaching assumes a less prominent role, but remains accessible to provide collaborative feedback and resources. Teams use the SIGs and pathways tools during their team collaboration on a consistent basis as a means to monitor and check the group's progress.

As teams eventually move to the unconscious competent stage, they solidify the routines of collective inquiry and develop habits of professional practice. These teams have often worked together for a longer period of time, and when they reflect, they are sometimes unable to dissect their team collaboration because it is so natural and engrained. These teams encourage divergent thinking, and trust among the team members is high. Teams in this stage are data-driven, serve as exemplary models of the PLC process, and are determined and focused on success for all students. They readily embrace cognitive conflict as the means to improve practice.

The coach at this stage is engaged in a process of gradual withdrawal and is present as often as the team requests. Teams view the coach as an equal and often ask the coach to join a meeting as a member of the group to offer ideas. The pathways are well established and the team utilizes the tool in the optimal manner.

Moving Through the Quadrants for Continuous Improvement

Teams operating in the unconsciously incompetent stage are unaware of the concept of continuous improvement, and they are not very interested in learning about it. The idea of sitting down and making a plan to study the effects of changes in their instructional practice can be a completely foreign idea. Teachers in this quadrant say, "It will take forever to do all this extra work; plus, I have always gotten good enough results with what I do in the classroom." These teams view the PDSA cycle as nothing more than a compliance activity and have not identified any of the specific tasks, created any routines, or established any habits in support of the notion of continuous improvement.

In this stage, the coaching role is mainly concerned with helping teams understand the importance of continuous improvement. Teachers need to understand that teaching is an ever-changing and evolving profession; thus, if the team does not continue improving, the logical consequence is that its professional practice will eventually become outdated and ineffective.

Teams operating in the consciously incompetent stage recognize that they should be working continuously to improve their professional practice but do not know how to approach the task. They have begun to identify the specific tasks that the team would need to do but do not have enough experience to engage in the process without some guidance or coaching. Identifying a problem of practice, planning the logistics of a pilot, and evaluating the impact of their improvement effort requires an extensive amount of time and energy from these teachers. Teams benefit from the step-by-step guidance the pathways provide, but without realizing it, they often skip or completely overlook important steps of the PDSA cycle.

These teams need small wins and encouragement; those in coaching roles can have a tremendous impact at this stage. Working side-by-side with the teams, coaches assist with identifying the problem, planning the logistics, and deciding what data to gather and analyze.

Teams operating in the consciously competent stage understand the importance of engaging in a process of continuous improvement, have sought out information and training, and strive to make it a regular and routine part of their work. These teams may need to set some norms as a reminder, but they can name and articulate the purpose of each steps in the PDSA cycle and are making a sincere effort to use it. Still, continuous improvement is hard work and requires a constant effort and attention.

It is not unusual for teams to become frustrated and give up after one or two rounds of the PDSA cycle, but coaches can help teachers refocus on what *is* working and what has changed for the better as a result of their efforts to improve.

Teams that reach the unconsciously competent stage have embraced the concept of continuous improvement and made it a part of the way their team operates. These teams are not deterred by occasional setbacks and persevere until they resolve the problem of practice. Teams at the unconsciously competent stage have identified the specific tasks within each step of the cycle, developed routines to help make the cycle more efficient and effective, and make a habit of moving through the steps of the PDSA cycle without thinking; it just comes naturally to them.

Coaches focus on helping unconsciously competent teams figure out their next steps by asking reflective questions and even encourage these teams to engage in some peer coaching to help other teams get better at the continuous improvement process.

Moving Through the Quadrants for Action Orientation

Unconsciously incompetent teams are not making connections to their dreams and visions with their everyday actions. They are unconscious about the kind of actions that create energy and momentum in their teaching and students' learning. They are unaware how team meetings energize and motivate those involved. They are also unaware that ineffective teams create disillusionment and inaction on the part of those involved. Teams in the unconsciously incompetent stage benefit from coaching moves like:

- Building a knowledge base on current reality
- Demonstrating how action connects to results (modeling)
- Creating products together to increase conceptual understanding
- Creating opportunities to learn about and reflect on practices in field visits and other classrooms
- Using action words and minimizing talk when it is time to act

As teams observe successful practices and start to engage in creating products they become consciously incompetent. These teams begin to realize that actions on their part will lead to better results for their students. They begin to feel a sense of urgency about current reality and understand what they do matters a great deal. They are conscious of the fact that if students are not successful, they may be part of the reason and take responsibility. Teams in this stage benefit from coaching around doing by:

- Helping teams create a short-term goals and design assessment strategies to check learning
- Following up by asking teams to talk about what they did and what they found
- Naming and celebrating specific successful actions
- Modeling transparency and talking about their own failures or attempts
- Publicly acknowledging those that are doing
- Providing just-in-time learning when the team is struggling

The consciously competent team uses meeting time for responding to the four critical questions of a PLC and defines actions and next steps during the meeting. They consistently use the same processes and practices and become efficient and effective. They know the steps they might use to deal with a challenge without referring to a tool and are comfortable with being impatient and having a sense of urgency.

Coaching at this stage should include:

- Sharing and talking about the PLC practices that make a difference
- Reinforcing evidence and success
- Providing opportunities for professional learning such as action research or applying to be a model PLC School (Visit All Things PLC [allthingsplc.info] for more information.)
- Creating opportunities for teams to share through learning fairs, writing an article or blog, presenting at a conference, or hosting visits from another school

The unconsciously competent team's work is routine, and the focus is truly student centered. The team uses the tools and structures of a PLC without hesitation. If faced with an obstacle, teams take it on with confidence and demonstrate a growth mindset. Coaching is about:

- Collecting stories to celebrate good work or to help a struggling team
- Providing recognition
- Using mediational questions to reflect on the learning

Moving Through the Quadrants for Results Orientation

When a team is unconsciously incompetent in the development of a results orientation, members are oblivious to the fact that focusing on results can improve student achievement. These teams teach instructional units and even measure students' progress, but they do not connect the two. They use assessment results to drive instruction because they don't realize they should. They teach, assess, give their students a grade, and move on to the next unit.

When a coach enters the scene and introduces the team to the school's SIG, the team begins to understand why using common assessments is a good idea. The coach continues to facilitate professional learning about the PLC process, and the team begins to realize members could be using evidence and samples of student work to identify those who need more time and support in mastering content. They do not yet possess the skills needed to analyze the data, so they can use it to inform instruction.

As the coach continues working with teams to build shared knowledge about PLCs, they engage in professional learning on assessment development and analysis. At this point, the team becomes consciously incompetent. The coach uses the pathways to guide the team through PLC question two, How will we know if our students have learned? Team members work collaboratively to develop their first common formative assessment based on essential standards and agree on the conditions for its administration. They bring the common formative assessment results to their next collaborative team meeting, and the coach guides them through a data-analysis protocol to determine which students need more time and support on specific learning targets. The team uses those results to develop an intervention plan for struggling students, and the coach encourages them to reflect on their own instructional practices. This team has become consciously competent as members diligently work to implement their new assessment-development and analysis skills to increase student achievement and improve instructional strategies.

As the coach guides the team and they practice these skills throughout the course of the school year, the process becomes more and more natural. Eventually, a results orientation becomes so ingrained in the team's everyday actions that it turns into a way of life. It is simply the way they do business. The team has developed a habit of practice in utilizing results to improve student achievement; they are unconsciously competent.

Moving Forward

By making ourselves aware of the learning stage each team currently occupies, coaches tailor their coaching to meet that team's needs. When combining this idea with identifying the appropriate coaching stance (consultant, collaborator, or reflective thinking), coaches increase the likelihood of successfully coaching collaborative teams to the next level of effectiveness. Adding the specificity of the four essential elements allows an even greater level of differentiation, providing coaches and teams the focus needed to make lasting and significant improvements.

A coach can wear the hat of the expert and operate in the role of *consultant* to help teams that are functioning in the unconscious incompetence stage. The coach's feedback in this situation takes on a more directive tone as he or she provides specific next steps. The instant clarity this provides can immediately shift a team to a positive trajectory.

For teams functioning in the conscious incompetence and conscious competence stages, a coach can take the stance of *collaborator* and dive in and work side by side with the team. This is the perfect opportunity to celebrate practices that are working and provide feedback that offers additional suggestions for improvement. Simply offering a new idea or two in this stage can help springboard teams to the next level of implementation.

As teams collaborate at increasingly high levels and function in the unconscious competence stage, a coach can take on a more *reflective stance*. Teams in this stage are in a prime space where a coach can provide feedback by posing questions to promote reflection and deepen learning. Teams that are unconsciously competent are able to make quick connections and readily move new thinking to action.

It is important to note that coaching stances do not correspond to Burch's Stages of Competence in a direct, one-to-one fashion. However, the use of these two processes, when combined, provide a powerful scaffold to coach teams.

While it is important to coach teams through the four stages of competency to improve their effectiveness as a PLC, it may be even more important that teams *believe* in themselves and their teammates' ability to improve student achievement. In chapter 8, we describe how coaching collaborative teams to develop habits of professional practice around the four essential elements of a PLC can positively impact the collective efficacy of the team, one of the most powerful influences in increasing student achievement.

Summary

- Each team is comprised of individuals; thus, implementation of the PLC process will vary due to human variables, such as the individual skills, personalities, and levels of commitment.
- Coaches should familiarize themselves with the research of Noel Burch (Adams, n.d.) and his four stages, which serves as a useful framework as coaches think about ways to support implementation of the PLC process.
- For a coach, being able to recognize specific behaviors in each of Burch's four stages will allow him or her to identify the current level of a team collaborative practice and move the team toward the next level of practice.

Reflection Questions

A coach plays an instrumental role in cultivating the conditions that are necessary for assessing a team's current reality. As you reflect on the content of this chapter, consider the following two questions.

1. Think about the teams you work with at your school. Choose one team and identify which of the four stages (which quadrant) reflects the team's current reality. Why did you choose this stage? What do you see and hear to support your decision?
2. Utilizing Burch's model, what is your next step to develop the specific behaviors, routines, and habits that will promote collective inquiry, continuous improvement, action orientation, and a focus on results?

CHAPTER 8

Believing in Your Team—Creating Collective Efficacy

The strength of the team is each individual member.
The strength of each member is the team.

—PHIL JACKSON

The essential elements of a PLC—collective inquiry, continuous improvement, action orientation, and results orientation—all work in tandem to help PLCs function at a high level, like a well-oiled machine. When this PLC engine is firing on all cylinders, an incredible synergy is created that results in a powerful element called collective efficacy. In this chapter, we explain how the intentional implementation of the PLC essential elements can help leaders develop collective efficacy among their collaborative teams.

Collective Efficacy

Have you ever attended a collaborative team meeting where teachers spend more time blaming students for poor assessment results than reflecting on their own practices? They cite factors such as low-socioeconomic status, lack of parental involvement, and student apathy for low achievement. While these are certainly difficult factors to overcome, research has shown there are ways to neutralize the impact of these issues. Researcher Albert Bandura (1993) finds that "the positive effects of CTE [collective teacher efficacy] on student academic performance more than outweigh the negative effects of low socioeconomic status" (cited in Brinson & Steiner, 2007, p. 1). In fact, the research of Hattie (2016) shows that high collective teacher efficacy can result in almost four times the amount of student growth one would expect to see in one year's time—almost *four times*! So, what exactly is collective efficacy and how do we produce it in our schools?

Brinson and Steiner (2007) describe collective teacher efficacy as "the perception of teachers in a school that the efforts of the faculty as a whole will have a positive effect on student learning" (p. 1). Jenni Donohoo (2017) describes it as "a staff's shared belief that through their collective action, they can positively influence student outcomes, including those who are disengaged and/or disadvantaged." When teachers have confidence in their ability as a team to positively impact student achievement, they possess collective teacher efficacy. And when they believe they can, they usually do. Dana Brinson and Lucy Steiner (2007) find that collective teacher efficacy not only leads to increased student achievement, but it also strengthens relationships between parents and teachers, creates a positive culture where teachers are committed to the school, and lessens the negative impact of low socioeconomic status.

Teachers with high levels of collective efficacy maintain a focus on learning rather than blaming outside factors for low achievement. They believe that all students can learn, despite negative social factors that may be impacting them. When comparing schools with similar demographics but varying levels of collective teacher efficacy, Brinson and Steiner (2007) find that "principals who work to build collective teacher efficacy will make greater strides toward closing the achievement gap in their schools" (p. 2). By paying attention to teachers' levels of efficacy and taking intentional steps to build it, school leaders move teachers and students both toward increased levels of achievement.

Collective Efficacy and PLCs

Schools that intentionally practice the essential elements of PLCs have a great start on building collective efficacy. Members of a PLC work collaboratively toward the common goal of high levels of learning for all students and have an intrinsic belief that, together with the team, they can actually make it happen. Members of PLCs maintain a focus on learning and ways to improve. They believe deeply in the need to continuously improve and engage in cycles of collective inquiry to test new ideas and examine their effectiveness. Rather than simply admitting to problems, PLC schools take action to solve those problems using best practice strategies that produce results. And finally, PLC members use results to guide instructional decisions and improve practice. These hallmark characteristics of a PLC all contribute to increased collective teacher efficacy.

When schools coach teams toward developing continuous improvement, collective inquiry, action orientation, and results orientation—essential elements of the PLC process—they increase the likelihood that teams will develop collective teacher efficacy. In fact, many studies have attempted to determine whether collective efficacy leads to high functioning PLCs or if high functioning PLCs result in high levels of collective efficacy (Goddard, Goddard, Kim, & Miller, 2015; Gray & Summers, 2015;

Kennedy & Smith, 2013; Lee, Dedrick, & Smith, 1991; Lee et al., 2011; Moolenaar, Sleegers, & Daly, 2012; Newmann, Rutter, & Smith, 1989; Rosenholtz, 1989). The results of these studies have been mixed on which element impacts the other, leading us to the conclusion that there is an undeniable reciprocity between the two.

A study by Robert Voelkel and Janet Chrispeels (2017) focuses on discovering whether a California school district's PLC process implementation led to an increase in teacher efficacy. (The study centered on a suburban California district with about 10,000 students that had been identified for program improvement before the implementation of PLCs). The answer, in this case, was a resounding "yes." Not only did these researchers find that effective PLCs led to increased collective teacher efficacy, but they conclude that school leaders should assist teams (we would argue they should *coach* teams) in the following areas:

- Setting clear, achievable goals;
- Analyzing student work
- Understanding how instruction shapes the student outcomes; and
- Using protocols to identify next instructional steps (Voelkel & Chrispeels, 2017, p. 521)

When we examine these recommendations closely, it is plain to see they all reflect the habits of highly effective teams.

How to Build Collective Teacher Efficacy

Research clearly shows there are specific factors that build a sense of collective efficacy (Bandura, 1986, 1993; Brinson & Steiner, 2007; Donohoo & Katz, 2017; Goodard, Hoy, & Hoy, 2004; Mulvey & Klein, 1998). In fact, Bandura (1997) identifies four specific sources of collective teacher efficacy: (1) mastery experiences, (2) vicarious experiences, (3) social persuasion, and (4) affective states. When schools operate as PLCs, they constantly and consistently provide opportunities for teachers to experience these four sources of collective efficacy.

Mastery Experiences

It has been said that success breeds success, and it is through successful experiences that coaches build the foundation for collective teacher efficacy. When a team accomplishes a goal, those members have participated in a mastery experience. They and their colleagues have done what they set out to do, which leaves them with a feeling of pride and accomplishment—especially when others recognize and celebrate those accomplishments. Team members have seen the positive impact their team can have, which motivates them to want to do more. On the other hand, failures can lower collective teacher efficacy, which is why leaders must coach collaborative teams toward mastery experiences.

Engagement in the four essential elements provides prime territory for teams to experience mastery. For example, when a team engages in a cycle of continuous improvement, members may identify a common problem of practice, apply a possible solution, and evaluate the quality of the solution. Whether the solution is successful or not, the team can experience mastery in the process of carrying out the collective inquiry cycle itself. "Collaborative teacher inquiry is a promising practice that can positively influence educators' interpretations of their effectiveness and thus enhance collective efficacy" (Donohoo & Katz, 2017, p. 22).

Likewise, maintaining a results orientation provides teams with opportunities to set goals for student achievement, measure progress, and celebrate success—a mastery experience. Voelkel & Chrispeels (2017) find that teams that set goals and analyze results to design interventions and examine teacher practices are predictive of higher collective teacher efficacy. Donohoo, Hattie, & Eells (2018) identify "evidence of impact" as a primary source of collective efficacy (p. 42). They encourage school leaders to help teachers connect student learning to teacher practice by analyzing assessment results and studying student work as a means of identifying effective instructional strategies. When leaders create a collaborative culture with expectations for a results orientation in a nonthreatening environment, "leaders have the potential to support school improvement in ways that positively influence teachers' collective efficacy beliefs and thus promote student achievement" (Donohoo et al., 2018, p. 42). Providing the additional structures and support for collaborative inquiry and action orientation allows teams to take the idea of a results orientation to an even deeper level, resulting in positive changes in teacher practices.

While some teams naturally develop mastery experiences on their own, it is the responsibility of school leaders to differentiate and scaffold learning for teams, so they can develop the habits of highly effective teams and begin to experience mastery themselves. It is also the job of leaders to help teams identify the small wins they might otherwise gloss over, and sincerely celebrate the accomplishments they have made. Charles Duhigg (2012) explains that small wins "fuel transformative changes by leveraging tiny advantages into patterns that convince people that bigger achievements are within reach" (p. 112).

By spending time coaching teams through the development of essential elements, we are far more likely to recognize when teams have accomplished those small wins, and we can use those mastery experiences to encourage our teams to keep moving forward and on to the next mastery experience.

Vicarious Experiences

Teams can derive collective teacher efficacy not only by experiencing mastery for themselves, but also by simply witnessing the success of others in comparable circumstances. This works because "when educators see others, who are faced with similar opportunities and challenges perform well, they come to expect that they, too, can succeed under similar conditions" (Donohoo & Katz, 2017, p. 23). When schools functioning as a PLC ask grade-level or content-area teams to share results with the rest of the faculty, they provide other teams with vicarious experiences. Staff members see that their colleagues, who operate under the same conditions with the same kinds of students, can be successful, and they begin to believe that they can also achieve positive results. PLCs consider celebration a priority, and strong PLC leaders find reasons to celebrate. Sharing in colleagues' successes not only strengthens the collaborative culture and feelings of collective responsibility, but it also boosts individual feelings of efficacy.

Similarly, teammates can provide each other with vicarious experiences that lead to increased efficacy. Collaborative teams in a PLC share individual classroom assessment results as a means of identifying successful practices. When one teacher achieves positive results and explains how she achieved them, she gives hope to others who may not have used that instructional strategy. The continual sharing of effective strategies in a PLC provides a natural platform for increasing collective teacher efficacy.

Likewise, whether it be through peer observations, instructional rounds, or learning labs, watching colleagues in action can be an incredible vicarious experience for building efficacy. When team members observe respected colleagues delivering instruction to students like their own, there is an extraordinary opportunity for deep, nonjudgmental conversation about topics such as the presenting teacher's intent, how the presenting teacher's practices compare with the observer's, and ways the presenting teacher overcame challenges, just to name a few. These opportunities allow the presenting teacher to reflect on his or her own practices while the observing teacher makes comparisons and identifies new methods.

When a coach facilitates these conversations, it strengthens even further the opportunity for deep analysis. Marzano (2011) states, "When teachers have an opportunity to observe and interact with their colleagues in a non-evaluative way regarding instruction, everyone wins" (p. 82). This type of vicarious experience is exactly what teachers need to build their confidence in their teammates, and in themselves. And when teachers have confidence in their teammates and themselves (collective efficacy), "there are significantly higher levels of academic achievement" (Donohoo et al., 2018). Remember, Hattie's (2016) research shows that high collective teacher efficacy results in almost four times the student growth we would expect to see in a single year of instruction.

Social Persuasion

In explaining social persuasion as a source of strengthening collective teacher efficacy, Donohoo and Katz (2017) define it as "individuals persuading one another that they constitute an effective team" (p. 23). PLCs are built on the foundation of teacher teams working collaboratively to ensure high levels of learning for all students. PLCs work to build a culture of collective responsibility. As teams become stronger through mastery and vicarious experiences, coaches can intentionally make statements to the team about their growing effectiveness as a means of building collective efficacy. As the leader or coach models this social persuasion, team members may begin to feel more comfortable verbalizing these ideas themselves.

Additionally, providing teams with specific feedback is a crucial part of coaching teams toward increased collective efficacy. Brinson and Steiner (2007) find that "high-quality, detailed performance feedback is necessary to build an organization with high collective efficacy that recognizes that it can face the challenges ahead" (p. 4). Effective PLC school leaders and coaches hold expectations and create conditions for teams to engage in the essential elements of PLCs while providing them with ongoing feedback and support. Utilizing the SIG allows a coach to gather specific evidence that indicates the team's current reality and can help the coach determine the types of feedback he or she provides. Further, using the Pathways for Coaching Collaborative Teams in a PLC can help coaches identify exactly which tasks teams have and have not engaged in regarding the four critical questions of a PLC, and can assist the coach in identifying the levels of support each team needs. This specific, detailed feedback is a crucial component of social persuasion in strengthening collective teacher efficacy.

In chapter 6, "Results Orientation," we spoke at length about the importance of principals and coaches meeting regularly with teams to discuss evidence of student learning. Not only do these conversations promote a results orientation, but they also encourage a sense of collective efficacy. Donohoo and associates (2018) find that "when instructional improvement efforts result in improved student outcomes that are validated through sources of student learning data, educators' collective efficacy is strengthened" (p. 41). When data shows the positive impact teachers have on student achievement, teachers tend to replicate those practices and collective efficacy is enhanced even further. When principals and coaches engage teachers in conversations about their data and ways to use evidence of student learning to inform future teaching, conversations begin to center on teacher reflection on instructional practices and away from forces over which teachers have little control. These conversations can be defined as social persuasion and a source of building collective teacher efficacy.

Affective States

The fourth source of efficacy relates to the emotional tone of the school or district. A high level of stress or anxiety can negatively impact the beliefs educators have in themselves and in their colleagues. When we let negative circumstances take over our thought processes, we have a tendency to downplay our own capabilities—and those of our students. When organizations fall into the trap of low collective efficacy, they engage in a cycle of learned helplessness: "School communities experience an inclination to stop trying, decreased expectations, and lower levels of performance" (Tschannen-Moran & Barr, 2004 as cited in Donohoo et al., 2018, p. 41). This leads to even lower levels collective efficacy, and the cycle continues.

However, schools with high levels of collective efficacy can withstand difficult challenges. "Since expectations for success are high, teachers and leaders approach their work with an intensified persistence and strong resolve" (Donohoo et al., 2018, p. 42). As teachers experience mastery, engage in vicarious experiences, and are exposed to positive social persuasion, they build a positive school culture and the foundation for high levels of collective efficacy. Feelings of excitement and pride motivate perceptions of the group's capabilities, triggering a desire to repeat positive performances. The goal of a PLC is to create a collaborative culture where we ensure high levels of learning for all students. When we work to intentionally create this positive culture, we lead our teams toward increased collective efficacy.

Moving Forward

Educators are constantly on the lookout for what works in schools. We continually search for the instructional strategies that will give us the biggest bang for our buck. The research of Hattie (2016) helps answer that question of what works by providing the effect sizes of strategies, conditions, and even materials we use to help increase student achievement. Hattie (2016) identifies collective efficacy as the most powerful factor impacting student achievement with an effect size at 1.57. And research shows that effective PLCs can lead to increased collective teacher efficacy. In fact, "a principal's instructional leadership significantly predicts collective efficacy by influencing teachers' collaborative work" (Donohoo & Katz, 2017, p. 26). It is our job, as educational leaders, to coach our collaborative teams toward mastery experiences, vicarious experiences, social persuasion, and positive affective states—the four sources of collective efficacy—through the essential elements of a PLC.

Summary

- Collective teacher efficacy is a faculty's perception that their efforts have a positive impact on student achievement (Donohoo, 2017; Goddard, Hoy, & Hoy, 2000).
- Collective teacher efficacy not only leads to increased student achievement, but it also strengthens relationships between parents and teachers, creates a positive culture where teachers are committed to the school, and lessens the negative impact of low socioeconomic status (Brinson & Steiner, 2007).
- There is an undeniable reciprocity between collective teacher efficacy and high-functioning PLCs.
- There are four sources of collective teacher efficacy: mastery experiences, vicarious experiences, social persuasion, and affective states (Bandura, 1997).
- When we operate as a PLC, we constantly provide opportunities for teachers to experience these four sources of collective efficacy.

Reflection Questions

A coach plays an instrumental role in cultivating the conditions necessary for collective efficacy. As you reflect on the content of this chapter, consider the following five questions.

1. How would you describe your faculty's current level of collective efficacy?
2. How do you provide your teachers with opportunities to experience mastery?
3. How are vicarious experiences a regular part of your teachers' practice?
4. What actions do you take to positively impact your school's affective state (climate)?
5. How do you use social persuasion to increase collective teacher efficacy?

CHAPTER 9

Creating an Action Plan for Coaching Collaborative Teams

People have built quite successful careers describing the hill, measuring the hill, walking around the hill, taking pictures of the hill, and so forth. Sooner or later, somebody needs to actually climb the hill.

—JEFFREY PFEFFER

The end of one school year is a great time to set goals for the next but setting goals is not the most important thing. In fact, setting goals without careful planning is just wishful thinking. The most successful principals, coaches, and teacher leaders set school improvement goals, make a plan to achieve their goals, and stick with it despite lots of distractions. They know a well-crafted improvement plan can keep their schools headed in the right direction long after the excitement of the first day of the new school year has passed.

Nearly all school-improvement planning follows a similar process: principals and teacher leaders review relevant data, involve members of the faculty to gather input, and reach consensus regarding potential goals. Members of the guiding coalition identify desired changes in teacher practice designed to bring about improved student achievement, determine specific administrative and faculty responsibilities, and carefully script a concise narrative explaining why accomplishing the proposed goals are so important. The best school improvement plans are concise by design, keep the number of goals limited, and utilize the SMART goal format to maximize the plan's potential impact.

In the context of coaching collaborative teams around improving their PLC practice, it is vital that coaches work with teams to co-create an action plan. Action plans focused on improving the essential elements of the PLC process help teams identify new behaviors, create efficient and effective routines, and promote development of productive habits of practice associated with collective inquiry, continuous improvement, an action orientation, and a focus on results.

When action plans are linked to an agreed upon standard of best practice (the SIG) and teams are provided the needed opportunities for coaching and support (the pathways) they are better able to describe what is expected in terms of team behaviors, establish ways to monitor the progress of teams, and determine the products that can be utilized as evidence to show growth. Improved teaching and learning are the natural consequences when coaches and teacher teams work collaboratively to align their talent and resources.

While the same basic process is applied to nearly any school improvement–planning process, the authors advocate an approach to implementing action plans based on the work of Dean Fixsen (2005). Throughout the rest of this chapter, using a framework developed by Fixsen (2005) and his colleagues as the lens, we will explore how those who coach collaborative teams can support and facilitate the development and execution of action plans. (See *Implementation Science: A Synthesis of the Literature* by Dean L. Fixsen, Sandra F. Naoom, Karen A. Blase, Robert M. Friedman, and Frances Wallace [2005] for more information on their work.) We pay special attention to the role coaches play in each stage of the implementation process.

As additional resources, the authors have also provided two tools coaches can use to support collaborative teams. The first is an action planning template. Doug Reeves (2011) argues the value of a school-improvement plan is inversely related to the length of the plan. Reeves (2007) cites evidence that "schools are well served by one-page plans that are clearly focused and simple enough that every participant in the process understands his or her role in executing the plan" (p. 87). Thus, the "Action Planning Template" (page 140) is designed to serve as a *plan on a page* and can be used equally well for planning at the district, school, or team level.

The second resource (appendix C) is a communication tool that can be used to develop a rollout plan for school-improvement plans. A rollout plan helps to (1) focus the planning process, (2) identify responsibilities for administrators and teachers, and (3) promote clarity about the various elements of an action plan. Our hope is that these tools, coupled with the explanation of an implementation process that follows, will allow coaches to have a greater impact on teacher teams in their schools.

Developed after years of experience, conducting research, and gathering evidence about the implementation process in complex organizations, Fixsen and his colleagues have created a theoretical framework that leaders can use to develop and implement action plans based on their school-improvement initiatives. The power of Fixsen's (2005) framework is in its elegant simplicity and our experience has been that using this framework as the basis for action planning dramatically increases the likelihood of success.

Fixsen's (2005) framework deconstructs the complexities of executing action plans into a series of six recursive stages which he labels (1) exploration, (2) installation, (3) initial implementation, (4) full implementation, (5) innovation, and (6) sustainability. While maintaining the underlying integrity of each stage, the authors have translated Fixsen's labels using vocabulary more familiar to those working in PLCs.

For our purposes, we refer to the six stages as (1) building shared knowledge, (2) generating collective commitments, (3) providing opportunities for learning about the work (guided practice), (4) providing opportunities for doing the work (independent practice), (5) encouraging conscious innovation, and (6) ensuring systemic sustainability. The coach's role in each of the six stages is reviewed in the following sections.

Stage 1: Building Shared Knowledge

In a PLC, the first thing teachers do is learn together. During this initial stage of implementation, principals, coaches, and teacher leaders work together to learn as much as possible about the proposed school-improvement initiative. When Building Shared Knowledge, teachers explore the research supporting the initiative and reach out to colleagues with similar experience—perhaps even visit other schools—in an effort to understand the potential impact the proposed changes will have on their classroom. According to Fixsen (2007), sharing information from a variety of sources and formats "is essential to increasing awareness of innovations and prompting professionals to consider the need to make changes in current practice" (p. 5).

At this stage the faculty and staff also confirm their current reality, reach consensus on the need for the proposed improvement initiative, create a powerful coalition to monitor progress of the work, and communicate a compelling vision of the future. These important tasks are typically the responsibility of the building's guiding coalition but leaders must remember that the single most important outcome of the first stage in any action planning process is that everyone understand the *why* behind what is being proposed.

Stage 2: Generating Collective Commitments

The second stage of Fixsen's framework is focused on the collective effort to generate a commitment to the successful execution of the action plan. This stage is where principals, coaches, and teacher leaders share how they intend to implement the action plan. Detailed descriptions of the who, what, when, where, and how, sometimes called the rollout plan, include things like the rationale supporting the need for this particular initiative, expectations and responsibilities of the faculty and administrators, and a schedule for training opportunities, plans for gathering feedback, and deadlines for the production of products. At this same time, an opportunity is provided for all stakeholders to raise concerns or offer suggestions for revising the action plan.

It is the leadership's responsibility at this point in the process to ensure that faculty and staff reach consensus on the proposed action plan. Understanding the definition of consensus may require that the faculty revisit the difference between unanimous agreement and consensus. In a PLC, consensus is reached when everyone has had a chance to say what they need to say and the will of the group is clear, even to those who most oppose it.

The most important outcome of this second stage, once the faculty and staff have reached consensus, is to generate a collective commitment amongst and between members of the faculty (or team) to do whatever it takes to promote the successful execution of the action plan.

Stage 3: Providing Opportunities for Learning About the Work (Guided Practice)

In the third stage, principals, coaches, and teacher leaders focus on providing professional development opportunities for teachers to learn about the proposed change. Those involved in coaching collaborative teams play a pivotal role by ensuring teacher teams have access to a variety of opportunities to learn. These may include, but should not be limited to, attending workshops and trainings, engaging in book studies and other professional reading, visiting other classrooms or schools, or simply having time to reflect on the work as part of their collaborative team meetings. The emphasis at this stage is on learning, learning, learning, and because teams are in the process of learning new skills, they will make mistakes. Coaches can help ensure that teacher teams feel safe about taking risks, trying new things, and learning together.

This stage of the action planning process is where most improvement initiatives fail because the work gets mired in process (learning) and never moves to actual practice (doing). This is also the time when resistance begins to emerge. By now, leadership has made it clear that the improvement initiative is a priority and at this stage of the process, principals, coaches, and teachers serving as part of the school's guiding coalition will inevitably encounter some push back from the faculty. Those involved in coaching collaborative teams should recognize, and be prepared to respond to, behaviors that are inconsistent with efforts to achieve agreed upon school-improvement goals.

The authors have identified three common forms of resistance that we call the *Ruler Test*, *Regression to the Meaningless*, and the *Goldilocks Syndrome*. All of these (the Ruler Test, Regression to the Meaningless, and the Goldilocks Syndrome) are nothing more than politically correct forms of resistance. Those in coaching roles should accept that some discomfort with the change will occur and is a natural part of the process.

One of the most common forms of resistance is the lack of willingness to take what we already know as best practice and implement it in our classrooms. This form of resistance is called the *Ruler Test* and it happens when we fail to bridge the knowing–doing gap in our schools. The best way to illustrate the Ruler Test is to hold a ruler, the kind typically found in any elementary classroom, to the side of your head. The Ruler Test refers to the twelve inches between the head (what we know) and the heart (what we are willing to do). Coaching plays a significant role in overcoming the Ruler Test. We already know what works and while recognizing that change is difficult, past practice and precedent should not be the reason for failing to engage in what we know is best practice. The challenge is to take what we already know and do things differently.

A second and very common form of resistance at this stage is called *Regression to the Meaningless*. This is a mythical correlate to the statistical construct of regression to the mean. Regression to the Meaningless occurs when teachers implement new curriculum, skills or practices at a superficial level.

When the process doesn't go as well as planned and impatience sets in, those working to improve their schools tend to back off of expectations as outlined in the original school-improvement plan. Implementation of the improvement plan stalls and the application of new skills or strategies never goes beyond the most inconsequential and cursory tasks. When Regression to the Meaningless happens, and only the simple or most easily accessible changes are made in classroom practice, schools become stuck in PLC lite. It takes time and attention to apply new learning in the classroom and here again, the ongoing support and encouragement of coaches in the form of specific feedback to teams, plays a huge role in ensuring that Regression to the Meaningless does not occur.

When the focus is on providing teachers with multiple opportunities to learn new curriculum, skills, or practices through training and coaching, some teachers will engage in another form of resistance referred to as the *Goldilocks Syndrome*. Named after the fairy tale, the Goldilocks Syndrome represents the request by resistors for more—or different—training in order to be successful. The Goldilocks Syndrome manifests itself in the call for different training at different times delivered in a different way, but the bottom line is that whatever level of training and support is provided, if the Goldilocks Syndrome is present, it will never be enough.

Those who coach collaborative teams should acknowledge that in the beginning, teachers may be uncomfortable with their levels of knowledge and expertise, but those same coaches should recognize that one of the critical moments in any school improvement journey is when teams shift the focus of their work from learning to doing. When the Goldilocks Syndrome is present, those coaching collaborative teams can actually celebrate because when teachers ask for more opportunities to improve their practice, it opens the door to other elements of the PLC process like collective inquiry, continuous improvement, action orientation, and a focus on results. It has been said that when Goldilocks visits, coaches know it is time to move on to the next stage of the action plan!

Stage 4: Providing Opportunities for Doing the Work (Independent Practice)

At this stage, the role of those coaching collaborative teams shifts from direct training to ongoing support, from learning about the new skills or strategies to actually doing them in the classroom. The most effective principals and coaches realize that if they continue to *only* provide training, they risk allowing the team to become trapped in the previous stage. At some point, teachers need to *just do it*!

An important component of this stage is providing the kind of coaching and support that will encourage teacher teams to reflect and make meaning of their practice. According to Jeanne Spiller, assistant superintendent for teaching and learning at Kildeer Countryside School District 96 in Buffalo Grove, Illinois, a key moment in a school district's journey to becoming a nationally recognized PLC "occurred when our teachers moved from 'learning' to 'doing.'" Spiller continued, "The focus of our professional development shifted from providing training to providing support [coaching] in areas where teachers needed it the most" (J. Spiller, personal communication, 2006).

As Michael Fullan (2010) says, "Capacity building is not just workshops and professional development. It is the daily habit of *working together*, and you can't learn this from a workshop or course. You need to learn it by doing it and having a mechanism for getting better at it on purpose" (p. 69). During this stage of the process, the goal of coaches is to ensure the new strategy or skill has been fully implemented and embedded into the school's culture.

Stage 5: Encouraging Conscious Innovation

Fixsen, Naoom, Blasé, & Wallace (2007) believe this stage of the framework is reached when four conditions exist. They encourage coaches and teams to resist the urge to innovate until most of the faculty and staff have (1) learned the new skill or strategy, (2) are able to use it with fidelity, (3) have used it long enough to understand the nuances of its application *and only then* should teams begin (4) working on improving the innovation itself.

Fixsen et al. (2007) cite "a growing body of evidence that shows implementation with fidelity produces benefits for consumers [teachers and students], while adaptation or reinvention leads to poor outcomes for consumers [teachers and students]" (p. 7). The lack of appreciation for the distinction between fidelity versus adaptation explains why schools that attempt to reinvent or rebrand the PLC process get stuck with PLC lite and, ultimately, fail to achieve the desired levels of improvement in student achievement.

Fixsen et al. (2007) emphasize the important role data play in determining which goals have been effective, add value, and deserve continued support. They argue, "Constructive change can occur in programs provided that improvements are based on data derived from attempts to implement innovations with fidelity in real world settings" (p. 7). The key phrase here is *with fidelity in real world settings.*

The most effective principals, coaches, and teacher leaders are constantly seeking opportunities to move teams from best practice to next practice. The sustainability of any new skill or strategy depends in large part on whether collaborative teams are "staying tuned in to the changes, anticipating the next set of changes, and continually maintaining high-fidelity services, even in the midst of continual change" (Fixsen et al., 2007, p. 7). At this stage, helping collaborative teams stay current in their pedagogy is an important responsibility of those in coaching roles.

When encouraging conscious innovation, collaborative teams are perfectly poised to embrace a culture of continuous improvement through the process of collective inquiry, action research, and a focus on results. Coaches should encourage teams to "first do it right, then do it differently" (Fixsen et al., 2007, p. 7). And, while coaches should encourage teacher teams to look for ways to tweak their practice to ensure better results, it is important to be clear that decision making must be based on data and reflect a results orientation.

Stage 6: Ensuring Systemic Sustainability

The work to ensure that learning new skills, executing new strategies, or implementing new curricula are systemically sustainable never ends. Fixsen et al. (2007) emphasize the importance of monitoring teams through "Ongoing quality assurance systems that include practical measures of outcomes positively impact sustainability" (p. 7). Just as coaching teams is the key to helping teachers create a working understanding of the new skill or strategy, so too is the role coaches play in building ongoing and sustained monitoring systems that support the next generation of best practice. In this stage, teachers become comfortable with being uncomfortable and embrace the idea of continuous improvement; the authors call this *being restless with your practice*.

At the end of any action planning process, school leaders should ask themselves three questions; let's consider them within the context of creating high performing collaborative teams. First, is the new skill or strategy embedded in the structure of our school? (Is every teacher a member of a meaningful team and is time for collaboration built into the regular school day?) Second, has the system created a critical mass of practitioners who have the necessary skills? (Are teacher teams able to respond to the four critical questions of a PLC with fidelity?) Third, is there a plan in place to provide the necessary support to new teachers who enter the system? (How do we intentionally help new teachers understand the value our school places on collaboration?)

Principals recognize that coaching collaborative teams can accelerate the development of a PLC in their school. They also understand that, as Rick DuFour (1998) states:

> If a change initiative is to be sustained, the elements of that change must be embedded within the culture of the school. Unless collective inquiry, collaborative teams, an orientation toward action, and a focus on results become part of "the way we do things around here," the effort to create a PLC is likely to fail. (p. 133)

Moving Forward

Creating an intentional action plan benefits any endeavor, whether you are climbing a mountain, losing weight, or implementing the PLC process in your school. In the context of coaching collaborative teams, co-created action plans define the forward trajectory targeted to improve PLC implementation. Teams that align action plans to an agreed-on standard of best practice (the SIG) and advocate for support and coaching (the pathways) are better suited to define their overall success. Action plans promote the development of productive habits of practice associated with collective inquiry, continuous improvement, an action orientation, and a focus on results.

Drafting and discussing an action plan is just the beginning. While an action plan defines the work, teams must also commit energy and time to doing the work. A well-crafted action plan is not designed to be a static document that lives in a binder somewhere on a shelf, but rather a dynamic document and process that supports change, growth, and possibilities. Embrace the work, and develop an action plan so that success is not left to chance.

Summary

- Setting school-improvement goals without creating the associated action plan typically results in the failure to improve teaching and learning in any meaningful way.
- Coaching collaborative teams can increase the likelihood that teams will successfully execute action plans.
- Action planning can be deconstructed into a series of manageable steps allowing teams to effectively engage in the school-improvement process.
- Coaches need to ensure that:
    - Teachers understand why execution of the action plan is important to improved teaching and learning
    - Everyone is committed to the success of the action plan
    - Teams have multiple opportunities, offered in a variety of ways, to learn new skills and strategies
    - Time is set aside for teachers to practice new skills and strategies in real life classroom settings
    - Innovation is based on data gathered from those same real life classroom settings
    - Plans are in place to help teachers and administrators new to the system understand the importance of executing the action plan

Reflection Questions

As you reflect on the content of this chapter, consider the following two questions.

1. Based on what you have learned, which of the six stages are teams operating at in your building? Cite evidence to support your claim.
2. Based on which one of the six stages teams are operating at in your building, what approach makes the most sense for those coaching collaborative teams?

APPENDIX A

Stages of Learning and Essential Elements of a Highly Effective PLC

Collective Inquiry

Quadrant 1: Teams Don't Know What They Don't Know

Tendencies:

- Teams resist working together or with a coach
- Teams rely on past practice
- Teachers attribute lack of results to students or external factors
- Decisions are based on individual preferences, perceptions, and opinions with limited inquiry or collaboration

Coaches can:

- Guide teams through an exploration of the collective inquiry SIG (page 54)
- Engage in professional learning focused on the purpose and benefits of collective inquiry

Possible products:

- Team reflections on professional learning
- Team self-evaluation on SIG

Quadrant 2: Teams Know What They Don't Know

Tendencies:

- Teams access and utilize data in a limited way
- Teams are compliant but often operate as individuals
- Trust among members may be low

Coaches can:

- Provide teams with professional learning and resources on the purpose and processes of collective inquiry
- Reference the SIG (pages 54–55) to help teams understand their next steps
- Utilize the pathways document (page 56) to help teams reflect on and move forward in the collective-inquiry process
- Model elements of collective inquiry processes
- Emphasize the seven norms of collaboration
- Shift language to a collective focus

Possible products:

- Team collective commitments regarding collective inquiry
- Team-identified collective-inquiry processes and protocols

Quadrant 3: Teams Know What They Know

Tendencies:

- Teams recognize that their practice is an ever-changing process
- Members view the collective intelligence of the team as the primary source of solutions for their students
- Teams utilize data to determine instructional success levels
- Members demonstrate respect, trust, and support for one another
- Teams respectfully challenge viewpoints and welcome cognitive dissonance as a vehicle for growth
- Research into best practice is a regular practice among members

Coaches can:

- Refer teams to the SIG and pathways as needed
- Point teams toward current research on best practices
- Ensure that teams are examining both external and internal evidence
- Encourage celebration when goals are met

Possible products:

- Team-identified topics for inquiry
- Team-identified collective inquiry processes and protocols
- Research-based solutions
- Results of collective inquiry cycles

Quadrant 4: Teams Don't Just Know It, They Live It!

Tendencies:

- Teams have solidified their agreed-on routines of collective inquiry so they have become habits of professional practice
- Divergent thinking is encouraged
- Trust among members is high
- Cognitive conflict is embraced as a means to improved practice
- Members consult current research along with internal evidence as a normal part of practice

Coaches can:

- Facilitate as the team requests
- Encourage celebration when goals are met

Possible products:

- Team-identified topics for inquiry
- Team-identified collective-inquiry processes and protocols
- Research-based solutions
- Results of collective inquiry cycles

Continuous Improvement

Quadrant 1: Teams Don't Know What They Don't Know

Tendencies:

- Teams are satisfied with the status quo and see no need for improvement
- Teams view the PDSA cycle as a compliance activity only

Coaches can:

- Provide teams with professional learning on the need for next practice
- Help teams understand the consequences of stagnant practice

Possible products:

- Professional development activities

Quadrant 2: Teams Know What They Don't Know

Tendencies:

- Teams recognize that they should be working continuously to improve their professional practice but do not know how to approach the task
- Teams begin to identify specific tasks for improvement but rely upon a coach to move them forward
- Teams may use the SIG or pathways to guide their work, but do not engage in the PDSA cycle

Coaches can:

- Provide teams with professional development on the specific steps of the PDSA cycle
- Walk teams through the process of identifying a problem of practice, planning logistics and deciding what data to gather and analyze
- Point out small wins and celebrate progress throughout the PDSA cycle
- Ask mediational questions, guiding teams to reflect on the process

Possible products:

- Identified problems of practice or tasks for improvement
- Team identified PDSA process

Quadrant 3: Teams Know What They Know

Tendencies:

- Teams strive to make continuous improvement a routine part of their work
- Teams can articulate the purpose of each step in the PDSA cycle and make a sincere effort to practice it
- Teams may become frustrated with the process but continue to move forward with the help of a coach

Coaches can:

- Collaborate with teams as they engage in each step of the PDSA cycle
- Help teams focus on the things that have changed for the better as a result of their quest for improvement
- Ask mediational questions, guiding teams to reflect on the process

Possible products:

- Documentation of the team's engagement in the PDSA cycle
- Reflection activities

4 Quadrant 4: Teams Don't Just Know It, They Live It!

Tendencies:

- Teams have embraced the concept of continuous improvement and made it a normal part of daily operation
- Teams have identified specific tasks within each step of the cycle and developed routines to make the cycle more efficient and effective

Coaches can:

- Assist teams as they decide on next steps by asking reflective questions
- Encourage teams to engage in peer coaching to help other teams improve their use of the PDSA cycle

Possible products:

- Documentation of the team's engagement in the PDSA cycle
- Reflection activities
- Peer coaching plans

Action Orientation

1 Quadrant 1: Teams Don't Know What They Don't Know

Tendencies:

- Teams do not make connections between the school's mission and their everyday actions
- Teams have little urgency in approaching their work
- Members do not understand the purpose of teams or collaboration
- Members may review data but rarely take action to improve results

Coaches can:

- Emphasize the connection between the school's mission and the work of the team
- Provide professional learning and resources on collaboration to improve student achievement
- Model urgency for response to student data
- Encourage teams to move from admiring data to acting upon it
- Use protocols and interactive strategies to facilitate collaborative work

Possible products:

- SMART goals
- Plans to meet SMART goals
- Protocols for responding to student data
- Processes and products for responding to the four critical questions

2 Quadrant 2: Teams Know What They Don't Know

Tendencies:

- Teams begin to realize that they can positively impact student achievement
- Members see that improving teaching practices could improve student learning, but do not know how to proceed

Coaches can:

- Assist teams in creating short term goals and plans for reaching them
- Ask teams to create products related to their work
- Provide professional learning on action research processes
- Ask teams to reflect on their actions and what they learned
- Model transparency through stories of failures that led to growth
- Celebrate the doing

Possible products:

- Rubrics, proficiency scales, common assessments, graphic organizers that reflect the team's work
- SMART goals and plans for reaching them
- Reflection activities

Quadrant 3: Teams Know What They Know

Tendencies:

- Teams spend meeting time responding to the four critical questions of a PLC with automaticity
- Team actions are efficient and effective
- The team is comfortable with a constant state of urgency

Coaches can:

- Reinforce the use of evidence that leads to success
- Provide feedback and support during the action research process
- Encourage reflective practices
- Create opportunities for celebration and sharing (such as learning fairs, presentations, publications, or application as a model PLC school)

Possible products:

- Meeting minutes responding to the four critical questions
- Data analysis and response documentation
- Intervention plans
- SMART goals and plans for meeting them
- Presentations and publications related to results

Quadrant 4: Teams Don't Just Know It, They Live It!

Tendencies:

- The team has an established routine for effectively and efficiently responding to the four critical questions of a PLC
- The team meets challenges with confidence and a growth mindset
- The team is constantly in a doing mode

Coaches can:

- Provide recognition of the good work being done
- Encourage celebration
- Ask mediational questions to encourage ongoing reflection
- Push for continuous improvement

Possible products:

- Meeting minutes responding to the four critical questions
- Data analysis and response documentation
- Intervention plans
- SMART goals and plans for meeting them
- Presentations and publications related to results

Results Orientation

1 Quadrant 1: Teams Don't Know What They Don't Know

Tendencies:

- Teams may be working toward district or school goals, but typically have not created grade-level or content-area SMART goals
- Teams are oblivious to the fact that focusing on results can improve student achievement
- Teachers teach, assess, give students a grade, and move on
- Program effectiveness is not considered

Coaches can:

- Utilize the SIG for results orientation (page 89) to build shared knowledge amongst the team
- Provide teams with resources and professional learning on the use of data to inform instruction

Possible products:

- Results orientation SIG self-evaluation
- Professional learning reflections

2 Quadrant 2: Teams Know What They Don't Know

Tendencies:

- The team begins to understand the end goal of common assessments.
- The team realizes they could be using assessment results to identify students who need more time and support in mastering content.
- Teachers recognize they need to make instructional and program improvements, but are unsure where to begin.

Coaches can:

- Ensure that teams have identified grade-level or content-area essential standards using a research-based protocol
- Assist team in developing short and long term SMART goals based on essential standards
- Provide teams with resources and professional learning on assessment creation and data analysis
- Support teams as they create common summative and formative assessments based on essential standards

Possible products:

- Grade-level or content-area essential standards
- SMART goal templates
- Common summative and formative assessments

3 Quadrant 3: Teams Know What They Know

Tendencies:

- Team members collaboratively develop SMART goals and use data to monitor progress toward the goals
- Team members collaboratively develop common summative and formative assessment based on essential standards and agree on the conditions for test administration
- Teams use data analysis protocols to analyze common formative and summative assessment results
- Teams utilize formative and summative assessment data to inform instruction and make plans for intervention and enrichment
- Teachers reflect upon and make adjustments to their own instructional practices
- Team members utilize data to reflect upon program effectiveness and make adjustments for future instruction

Coaches can:

- Guide teams in the collection of progress monitoring data for SMART goals
- Help ensure that common assessments are aligned to essential standards at appropriate levels of rigor
- Provide teams with options for data analysis protocols

- Encourage teams to explore intervention and enrichment strategies they may not have used before
- Ask mediational questions to support individual teacher reflection for instructional improvement
- Ask mediational questions to support reflection upon program effectiveness
- Help make plans for program improvement based on data

Possible products:

- SMART goal templates
- Common summative and formative assessments aligned with essential standards at appropriate levels of rigor
- Data analysis protocols
- Intervention and enrichment plans based on data analysis
- Teacher reflection documents
- Program improvement documentation

Quadrant 4: Teams Don't Just Know It, They Live It!

Tendencies:

- Teams regularly create and deliver common formative and summative assessments as a part of each instructional unit
- Teams regularly utilize data analysis protocols that are carried out seamlessly in an effort to identify students who need more time and support
- Teams use data analysis results to collaboratively develop intervention plans for struggling students
- Teachers are naturally self-reflective and continually use assessment data and student work analysis to improve instructional practices
- Team members utilize data and student work analysis to reflect on program effectiveness and make adjustments for future instruction

Coaches can:

- Keep teams abreast of new intervention and enrichment strategies
- Ask mediational questions to support individual teacher reflection for instructional improvement
- Ask mediational questions to support reflection upon program effectiveness
- Assist with program improvements as needed

Possible products:

- Ever-evolving intervention and enrichment plans based on individual student data
- Reflection activities and documentation
- Program improvement documentation

APPENDIX B

Action Planning

Action-Planning Template

Progress Checkpoints	10 Days From Now	20 Days From Now	40 Days From Now	80 Days From Now	90 Days From Now	100 Days From Now
Checkpoint Date						
Stage of PLC Implementation	Build Shared Knowledge	Develop Collective Commitments	Provide Opportunities for Guided Practice	Provide Opportunities for Independent Practice	Innovate and Continuously Improve	Sustain Improved Levels of PLC Practice
Desired Outcomes: Describe the specific actions at each stage that are required to accomplish your goal.						
Team Behavior: What changes in practice are anticipated as a result of the actions?						
Progress Monitoring: How will you measure and monitor progress? How often?						
Artifacts: What evidence will be collected?						

Coaching Collaborative Teams in a PLC at Work: PLC 100-Day Plan Implementation Checkpoints

The 100-Day Plan Implementation Checkpoints section is a co-created, one-page, benchmarked plan. It details the components required to successfully accomplish the prioritized next step and resulting SMART goal that we identified in part I. While the format appears linear, implementation is a complex process and requires flexibility to move back and forth between steps as teams strive to improve.

When a system is clear and actualizes each key component on the left side of figure B.1, the probability of improved effectiveness of collaboration increases. It is equally important to build shared knowledge, develop collective commitments, provide guided practice, provide opportunities for independent practice, innovate and continuously improve, and sustain improved levels of PLC practice for each of the components. This ensures common understanding and expectations are in place so teams successfully achieve their goal or prioritized next step.

<table>
<tr><td colspan="2">Feedback: Once the plan is completed and teams work to meet their goal, ensuring timely, relevant, and actionable feedback is the catalyst to ensure success. Use this one-page document to capture possible feedback to be offered to the team.</td></tr>
<tr><td rowspan="2">Desired Outcomes: Describe the specific actions at each stage that are required to accomplish your goal.
Team Behavior: What changes in practice are anticipated as a result of the actions?
Progress Monitor: How will you monitor impact and results of these action steps on student learning? What is the intentional process and timeline? Who will be involved?</td><td>Building Shared Knowledge
• What do we need to think about and explore to reach our outcome?
• What common learning is required and how will we access it?
• What are some possible challenges?
• What past practice has proven successful? How can it be built on?
• Is there an expert or exemplar to support the work?</td></tr>
<tr><td>Develop Collective Commitments
• What team actions and behaviors need to be demonstrated to ensure the goal is met?
• What commitments will be made to each other?
• How will incongruent actions and behaviors be addressed?</td></tr>
</table>

Figure B.1: 100-day plan implementation checkpoints.

continued →

<table>
<tr>
<td rowspan="4">Artifacts: What evidence will be collected?
What are you specifically looking for in the artifacts? (For example, for each unit, teams will create at least one common formative and one common end of unit assessment tied to essential learning targets.)
Feedback: Once the plan is completed and teams work to meet their goal, ensuring timely, relevant, and actionable feedback is the catalyst to ensure success, use this one-page document to capture possible feedback to offer to the team.</td>
<td>Provide Opportunities for Guided Practice:<ul><li>Who will support implementation?</li><li>What current support structures are available?</li><li>Based on the goal, what new structures might need to be considered?</li><li>How will individuals access support?</li><li>How might the impact of the support be determined?</li><li>What suggestions or modeling needs to be considered?</li></ul></td>
</tr>
<tr>
<td>Provide Opportunities for Independent Practice<ul><li>What are your next steps?</li><li>How do you know they are your next steps?</li><li>What type of coaching support will be required?</li><li>How will the three feedback stances be utilized to offer support?</li><li>When will misconceptions be addressed?</li></ul></td>
</tr>
<tr>
<td>Innovate and Continuously Improve<ul><li>What will be investigated to expand on what you know?</li><li>We now understand how to . . .</li><li>We were surprised by . . .</li><li>We are beginning to wonder why . . .</li><li>We see connections between . . .</li><li>We would like help with . . .</li></ul></td>
</tr>
<tr>
<td>Sustain Improved Levels of PLC Practice<ul><li>What are some obstacles we may encounter?</li><li>Based on what works, how shall we move forward?</li><li>Based on what we have learned how will capacity be built across the system?</li><li>How will lessons we have learned be shared with others?</li><li>How will those new to the organization be onboarded into current practice?</li></ul></td>
</tr>
</table>

APPENDIX C

Communicating the Action Plan

Directions for Preparing An Action Plan

Part I: Assessing Current Practice and Prioritizing Next Steps

Section 1.1 Action Plan: Potential Areas of Improvement

Use the PLC strategy implementation guide to explore the anchor statements and associated indicators. Have a conversation about each anchor and indicator.

1. Code the indicators on the strategy implementation guide:
    a. What is solid and in place? How do you know?
    b. What is in process?
    c. Where are you stuck?
    d. What do you see as topics to tend to?
2. Based on your highlights, consider the overarching trends and themes:
    a. Where are your highest leverage points that will increase:
        - PLC implementation to the next highest indicator level?
        - Teachers and student learning and results?
    b. As a team, reach consensus on two or three potential areas you will need to focus on to deepen PLC implementation.

Action Step: Fill in the Potential Area of Improvement sections on the Action Planning Form for Part I (page 152), using the language from specific indicators or combine multiple indicators in a way that makes sense to you.

Section 1.2 Action Plan: Highest-Priority Next Step

1. Based on the potential areas for improvement identified in section 1.1, reach consensus on one that holds the greatest potential to increase PLC practice and leverage the effectiveness of the team. Consider, does the prioritized next step:
    a. Strike the right balance of effectiveness and efficiency?
    b. Identify and implement those strategies that have the greatest potential impact to improve teaching and learning?
    c. Build on a current area of strength?

Action Step: On the Action Planning Form for Part I (page 153), fill in the Highest-Priority Next Step section.

Section 1.3 Action Plan: Theory of Action

1. Collectively draft an If . . . Then . . . statement for your prioritized next step.
    a. Make an intentional connection between your prioritized next step and the intended team PLC outcomes you hope you achieve.
    b. Connect the outcomes to team actions and behaviors as well as student learning outcomes.

c. Confirm whether the Theory of Action statement communicates relevance and explain why your prioritized next step is essential.

Action Step: On the Action Planning Form for Part I (page 153), fill in the Theory of Action section.

Section 1.4 Action Plan: SMART Goal

1. Compare your prioritized area of need to the PLC pathway document. As a team, use evidence to reflect on the inquiry questions and determine which question best captures a specific next step.
    a. Convert the question into a team SMART goal that is specific, measurable, attainable, results oriented, and time bound.

Action Step: On the Action Planning Form for Part I (page 153), fill in the SMART Goal section.

Part II: Identifying the Responsibilities for the Faculty or Team

Section 2.1 Action Plan: Next Steps and SMART Goal

1. Faculty Expectations
    a. Brainstorm: What will the faculty or team need to commit to in order to meet the SMART goal at the end of 100 days?
    b. Have you considered setting faculty or team expectations and commitments for:
        i. Ongoing learning and engagement in a collaborative team coaching process?
        ii. Developing a 100-day plan?
        iii. Sharing the details and progress of the plan with administration and other key stakeholders?
        iv. An ongoing communication structure to inform the system of successes and challenges?
        v. Scheduling regular times to collaborate?
        vi. Monitoring the goal and conducting progress checks?
        vii. Identifying successes and celebrating?
        viii. Intentionally connecting the goal to the school mission, vision, and collective commitments?
        ix. Revisiting team structures?
        x. Revisiting the seven norms of collaboration?
        xi. Collecting tangible evidence demonstrating progress? (For example, team observation notes, templates, prioritized standard, unwrapping template, common assessments, data trackers, and so on)

Action Step: Based on your conversation, fill in the Faculty or Team Expectations column of the Action Planning Form for Part II (page 154).

2. Resources
    a. Are there internal resources that faculty or team can access to support the work toward their goal?
    b. What resources exist elsewhere in the system?
    c. What evidence-based research and books are available to investigate?
    d. Do other schools' websites hold possible solutions?

Action Step: Based on your conversation, fill in the Resources column of the Action Planning Form for Part II (page 154).

3. Persons Responsible
    a. While all team members participate and support the 100-day plan goal, the person responsible takes the lead to ensure a clear and ongoing focus.
    b. Are there different components of the plan where certain faculty or team members hold content or process expertise?

Action Step: Based on your conversation, fill in the Persons Responsible column of the Action Planning Form for Part II (page 154).

4. Timeline
    a. What is a reasonable timeline for each action item?

Action Step: Based on your conversation, fill in the Timeline column of the Action Planning Form for Part II (page 154).

Part III: Identifying the Responsibilities for the Administration

Section 3.1 Action Plan: Based on Highest-Priority Next Step and SMART Goal

1. Administrative Expectations
    a. Brainstorm: What is everything administration will need to commit to in order to meet the goal at the end of 100 days?
    b. Have you considered setting administrative expectations for:
        i. Teams learning and engagement in a collaborative team coaching process?
        ii. Sharing with faculty the details and importance of developing and committing to a 100-day plan?
        iii. Meeting with teams to monitor progress on their 100-day plans?
        iv. Providing professional learning for the entire faculty while differentiating learning based on individual team needs?
        v. Identifying successes and celebrating?
        vi. Monitoring mission, vision, and collective commitments?
        vii. Monitoring team structures?
        viii. Monitoring artifacts and products that demonstrate progress?

Action Step: Based on your conversation, fill in the Administrative Expectations column of the Action Planning Form for Part III (page 155).

2. Resources
    a. How will you collect trends and patterns (formal and informal) to determine common learning needs?
    b. How will you monitor and differentiate the support and learning each team needs to meet their goal?
    c. Are there internal resources that the faculty or team can access to support work toward their goal?
    d. What resources exist elsewhere in the system?
    e. What evidence-based research and books are available to investigate?
    f. Are there other schools or websites that they can access that have potential solutions?

Action Step: Based on your conversation, fill in the Resources column of the Action Planning Form for Part III (page 155).

3. Persons Responsible
    a. How will administration monitor the implementation of 100-day plans and who will be assigned to take the lead to monitor and support specific teams?

   b. Do certain administrators hold content or process expertise that can benefit certain teams and their goals?

Action Step: Based on your conversation, fill in the Persons Responsible column of the Action Planning Form for Part III (page 155).

4. Timeline

   a. How often will you monitor and check on team progress? Do all teams require a similar timeline?

Action Step: Based on your conversation, fill in the Timeline column of the Action Planning Form for Part III (page 155).

Part IV: Preparing the Message

Section 4.1 Action Plan: Purpose (Why)

Creating a common *why* with your guiding coalition is foundational to a strong communication plan. Consider the following questions or sentence starters to craft your collective purpose (objective or *why*).

1. Explain why coaching PLC collaborative teams matters, why is it important, and specifically why the school or team should engage in this work.
2. Why is the implementation of this plan necessary?
3. Identify the purpose of PLCs for your school.
4. Why do you want to achieve this objective?

Action Step: Based on your conversation, create statements that align to your common purpose using the Action Planning Form for Part IV (page 156).

Section 4.2 Action Plan: Empowering Description (What)

Create an inspiring, positive description of the actions that you, the team, and the school will engage in to ensure the success of your PLC and collaborative teams. Remember, as you create this description, it should be energizing!

1. Describe in vivid detail what you envision your school or team will look like when this plan is completed.
2. What changes do you expect?
3. How will your school and student learning be different?
4. What elements of school life will be the same? Not everything is changing.

Action Step: Based on your conversation, create an empowering description to share with your stakeholders using the Action Planning Form for Part IV (page 156).

Section 4.3 Action Plan: Audience (Who, When, and Where)

Knowing your audience will help you create a plan to communicate your purpose and your vision. Draw upon your collective knowledge about your school's culture, team dynamics, and individual styles as you consider conditions to create a favorable environment to share your message.

1. Who are you trying to reach?
2. Will there need to be different messages to various teacher teams?
3. When is an optimal time to share the message?
4. What might you need to consider in regard to obstacles?
5. How will you react or re-message if the message is not accepted?

Action Step: Based on your conversation, list when and where and to whom you will communicate your plan using the Action Planning Form for Part IV (page 156).

Section 4.4 Action Plan: Purposeful Plan for Communicating (How)

No plan has ever improved anything. It is the people who put the plan in motion that make the difference. Design a conscious, detailed, intentional communication plan that considers:

1. Purpose—section 4.1 (p. 156)
2. Vision—section 4.2 (p. 156)
3. Audience—Section 4.3 (p. 156)

Action Step: The desired result is a strong communication plan for coaching collaborative teams. Collectively determine how you will pull it all together, and fill in section 4.4 on the Action Planning Form for Part IV (page 156).

Action Planning Form for Part I

District, School, or Team ______________________________

Part I: Assessing Current Practice and Prioritizing Next Steps

Section 1.1 Action Plan: Potential Areas of Improvement

Based on evidence regarding the current level of PLC practice, use the SIG anchor statements and indicators to identify three areas where improvement in PLC processes, practices, and behaviors would lead to higher levels of learning for all students.

SIG potential area of improvement: Evidence or observation that this is an area of need:
SIG potential area of improvement: Evidence or observation that this is an area of need:
SIG potential area of improvement: Evidence or observation that this is an area of need:

Section 1.2 Action Plan: Highest-Priority Next Step

Provide a rationale for choosing this as a leverage point.

Section 1.3 Action Plan: Theory of Action

Write a theory of action to address the prioritized next step.

If . . . Then . . .

Section 1.4 Action Plan: SMART Goal

Use the pathways inquiry questions to write a SMART goal to support the theory of action.

Action Planning Form for Part II

District, School, or Team ____________________

Part II: Identifying the Responsibilities for the Faculty or Team

2.1 Action Plan: Based on Highest-Priority Next Step and SMART Goal

Use the SIG and pathway indicators and descriptors to detail implementation expectations for faculty.

Faculty or Team Expectations	Resources	Persons Responsible	Timeline

Action Planning Form for Part III

District, School, or Team ___________________________

Part III: Identifying the Responsibilities for the Administration

Section 3.1 Action Plan: Based on Highest-Priority Next Step and SMART Goal

Use the strategy implementation guide and pathways to detail implementation expectations for administration.

Administrative Expectations	**Resources**	**Persons Responsible**	**Timeline**

Action Planning Form for Part IV

District, School, or Team ____________________

Part IV: Preparing the Message

Section 4.1 Action Plan: Purpose (Why)

Section 4.2 Action Plan: Empowering Description (What)

Section 4.3 Action Plan: Audience (Who, When, and Where)

Section 4.4 Action Plan: Purposeful Plan for Communicating (How)

REFERENCES AND RESOURCES

Adams, L. (n.d.). *Learning a new skill is easier said than done.* Accessed at gordontraining.com /free-workplace-articles/learning-a-new-skill-is-easier-said-than-done/ on October 3, 2019.

AllThingsPLC. (2016). *Glossary of key terms and concepts.* Accessed at www.allthingsplc.info /files/uploads/Terms.pdf on October 1, 2019.

Amah, E., Nwuche, C. A., & Chukuigwe, N. (2013). Result oriented target setting and leading high-performance teams. *Industrial Engineering Letters, 3*(9), 47–59.

Anderson, D. L., & Anderson M. C. (2005). *Coaching that counts: Harnessing the power of leadership coaching to deliver strategic value.* Burlington, MA: Elsevier Butterworth-Heinemann.

Bambrick-Santoyo, P. (2012). *Leverage leadership: A practical guide to building exceptional schools.* San Francisco: Jossey-Bass.

Bandura, A. (1986). *Social foundations of thought and action: A social cognitive theory.* Englewood Cliffs, NJ: Prentice-Hall.

Bandura, A. (1993). Perceived self-efficacy in cognitive development and functioning. *Educational Psychologist, 28*(2), 117–148.

Bandura, A. (1997). *Self-efficacy: The exercise of control.* New York: Freeman.

Best, J., & Dunlap, A. (2017). *Continuous improvement in schools and districts: Policy considerations.* Denver, CO: McREL International.

Bolam, R., McMahon, A., Stoll, L., Thomas, S., & Wallace. M. (2005). *Creating and sustaining effective professional learning communities* (Research Report No. RR637). London: Department of Education and Skills. Accessed at www.education.gov.uk/publications /eOrdering Download/RR637–2.pdf on September 8, 2018.

Bridges, W., & Mitchell, S. (2000). Leading transition: A new model for change. *Leader to Leader, 16*(3), 30–36.

Brigham, S. E. (1994). TQM: Lessons we can learn from industry. In *Quality goes to school: Readings in total quality management in education.* Arlington, VA: American Association of School Administrators.

Brinson, D., & Steiner, L. (2007). *Building collective efficacy: How leaders inspire teachers to achieve.* Washington, DC: The Center for Comprehensive School Reform and Improvement.

Bolam, R., McMahon, A., Stoll, L., Thomas, S., & Wallace, M. (2005). *Creating and sustaining effective professional learning communities.* London: Department of Education and Skills. Accessed at dera.ioe.ac.uk/5622/1/RR637.pdf on September 8, 2018.

Buchanan, G. (n.d.). *Developing a coaching culture within your organization.* Accessed at theundercoverrecruiter.com/developing-a-coaching-culture/ on July 6, 2019.

Chang-Wells, G. L., & Wells, G. (1997). Modes of discourse for living, learning and teaching. In S. Hollingsworth (Ed.), *International action research: A casebook for educational reform* (pp.147–156). London: Falmer Press.

Chong, C. (2015). *Blockbuster CEO once passed up a chance to buy Netflix for only $50 million.* Accessed at www.businessinsider.com/blockbuster-ceo-passed-up-chance-to-buy-netflix-for-50-million-2015-7 on August 23, 2019.

Clear, J. (2015, April 29). *Habit stacking: How to build new habits by taking advantage of old ones* [Blog post]. Accessed at www.huffingtonpost.com/james-clear/what-is-habit-stacking_b_6738954.html on August 7, 2018.

Clutterbuck, D., & Megginson, D. (2005). *Okay the three of 214.* London: CIPD.

Conzemius, A. E., & O'Neill, J. (2002). *The handbook for SMART school teams.* Bloomington, IN: Solution Tree Press.

Donohoo, J. (2017, January 9). *Collective teacher efficacy: The effect size research and six enabling conditions* [Blog post]. Accessed at http://thelearningexchange.ca/collective-teacher-efficacy/ on September 24, 2019.

Donohoo, J., Hattie, J., & Eells, R. (2018). The power of collective efficacy. *Educational Leadership, 75*(6), 40–44.

Donohoo, J., & Katz, S. (2017). When teachers believe, students achieve: Collaborative inquiry builds teacher efficacy for better student outcomes. *Learning Professional, 38*(6), 20–27.

Donohoo, J., & Velasco, M. (2016). *The transformative power of collaborative inquiry: Realizing change in schools and classrooms.* Thousand Oaks, CA: Corwin Press.

DuFour, R. (2015). *In praise of American educators: And how they can become even better.* Bloomington, IN: Solution Tree Press.

DuFour, R., DuFour, R., Eaker, R., & Karhanek, G. (2004). *Whatever it takes: How professional learning communities respond when kids don't learn.* Bloomington, IN: Solution Tree Press.

DuFour, R., DuFour, R., Eaker, R., & Many, T. W. (2006). *Learning by doing: A handbook for Professional Learning Communities at Work.* Bloomington, IN: Solution Tree Press.

DuFour, R., DuFour, R., Eaker, R., Many, T., & Mattos, M. (2016). *Learning by doing: A handbook for Professional Learning Communities at Work* (3rd ed.). Bloomington, IN: Solution Tree Press.

DuFour, R., & Eaker, R. (1998). *Professional Learning Communities at Work: Best practices for student achievement.* Bloomington, IN: Solution Tree Press.

Duhigg, C. (2012). *The power of habit: Why we do what we do in life and business.* New York: Random House.

Eaker, R., & Dillard, H. (2017, Fall). Why collaborate? Because it enhances student learning! *AllThingsPLC Magazine*, 46–47.

East, K. A. (2015). A study of professional learning communities: Characteristics of implementation and perceived effectiveness in improvement schools in West Virginia. *Theses, Dissertations and Capstones*, 937.

Elgart, M. A. (2017). Can schools meet the promise of continuous improvement? *Phi Delta Kappan, 99*(4), 54–59.

Evans, N. J. (2011). The argument against coaching cultures. *International Journal of Coaching in Organizations*, 30, *8*(2), 35–48.

Fixsen, D. L., Naoom, S. F., Blasé, K. A., Friedman, R. M., & Wallace, F. (2005). *Implementation research: A synthesis of the literature* (Florida Mental Health Institute Publication #231). Tampa, FL: University of South Florida, Louis de la Parte Florida Mental Health Institute.

Fixsen, D. L., Naoom, S. F., Blasé, K. A., & Wallace, F. (2007). Implementation: The missing link between research and practice. *APSAC Advisor, 19*(1,2), 4–11.

Forbes Coaches Council. (2016). *13 Ways leaders can build a coaching culture at work.* Accessed at www.forbes.com/sites/forbescouchingcounsel/2016/10/0 66/13 –ways –leaders–can–build–a-coaching–culture–at–Work/#65b9d13544b6 on June 30, 2019.

Fullan, M. (2008). *The six secrets of change.* San Francisco: Jossey-Bass.

Fullan, M. (2010). *All systems go: The change imperative for whole system reform.* Thousand Oaks, CA: Corwin Press.

Fullan M., & Quinn, J. (2016). *Coherence: The right drivers in action for schools, districts, and systems.* Thousand Oaks, CA: Corwin Press.

Garmston, R. J., & Wellman, B. M. (2013). *The adaptive school: A sourcebook for developing collaborative groups* (2nd ed.). Lanham, MD: Rowman and Littlefield.

Garmston, R. J., & Wellman, B. M. (2016). *The adaptive school: A sourcebook for developing collaborative groups* (3rd ed.). Lanham, MD: Rowman and Littlefield.

Garmston, R. J., Wellman, B. M., Dolcemascolo, M., & McKanders, C. (2016). *Adaptive schools foundation seminar learning guide.* Moorabbin, Australia: Hawker Brownlow Education.

Goddard, R., Goddard, Y., Kim, E. S., & Miller, R. (2015). A theoretical and empirical analysis of the roles of instructional leadership, teacher collaboration, and collective efficacy beliefs in support of student learning. *American Journal of Education, 121*(4), 501–530.

Goddard, R. D., Hoy, W. K., & Hoy, A.W. (2000). Collective teacher efficacy: Its meaning, measure, and impact on student achievement. *American Educational Research Journal, 37*(2), 479–507.

Goddard, R. D., Hoy, W. K., & Hoy, A.W. (2004). Collective efficacy beliefs: Theoretical developments, empirical evidence, and future directions. *Educational Researcher, 33*(3), 3–13.

Goldberg, M. C. (1998). *The art of the question: A guide to short-term question-centered therapy*. New York: Wiley.

Gordon, T., & Burch, N. (1977). *T.E.T. teacher effectiveness training, instructors guide*. New York: David McKay.

Gorenflo, G., & Moran, J. W. (2010). *The ABCs of PDCA*. Washington, DC: Public Health Foundation.

Gormley, H., & van Nieuwerburgh, C. (2014). Developing coaching cultures: A review of the literature. *Coaching: International Journal of Theory, Research and Practice, 7*(2), 90–101.

Gray, J. A., & Summers, R. (2015). International professional learning communities: The role of enabling school structures, trust, and collective efficacy. *International Education Journal: Comparative Perspectives, 14*(3), 61–75.

Greene, K. (2018). A coach for every teacher. *ASCD Education Update, 60*(3), 1–5.

Guskey, T. R. (2000a). *Evaluating professional development*. Thousand Oaks, CA: Corwin Press.

Guskey, T. R. (2000b). Grading policies that work against standards . . . and how to fix them. *NASSP Bulletin, 84*(620), 20–29.

Hasselbein, F., & Johnston, R. (Eds.) (2002). *On leading change: A leader to leader guide*. San Francisco: Jossey-Bass.

Hattie, J. (2009). *Visible learning: A synthesis of over 800 meta-analyses relating to achievement*. New York: Routledge.

Hattie, J. (2012). *Visible learning for teachers: Maximizing impact on learning*. New York: Routledge.

Hattie, J. (2016, July). *Mindframes and maximizers*. Paper presented at the third Annual Visible Learning Conference in Washington, DC.

Hawkins, P. (2012). *Creating a coaching culture*. Maidenhead, England: Open University Press.

Heifetz, R., & Linsky, M. (2002). *Leadership on the line*. Boston: Harvard Business School Press.

Hord, S. M., Rutherford, W. L., Huling-Austin, L., & Hall, G. E. (1987). *Taking charge of change*. Alexandria, VA: Association for Supervision and Curriculum Development.

Horton, A. (2018). *Why are you still here? Inside the last Blockbuster in America*. Accessed at www.washingtonpost.com/news/business/wp/2018/07/14/why-are-you-still-here-inside-the-last-blockbuster-left-in-america/?noredirect=on on August 23, 2019.

International Coaching Federation. (2014). *Building a coaching culture.* Accessed at www.performanceconsultants.com/coaching-culture on June 30, 2019.

International Coaching Federation. (2017). *Building a coaching culture with millennial leaders.* Accessed at www.performanceconsultants.com/coaching-culture on June 30, 2019.

International Coaching Federation. (2018). *Creating a coaching culture for change management.* Accessed at www.performanceconsultants.com/coaching-culture on June 30, 2019.

Jenkins, W. (2018). *Coaching starts with creating a collaborative culture.* Accessed at www.td.org/insights/your-coaching-starts-with-creating-a-collaborative-culture on July 6, 2019.

Katz, S., & Dack, L. A. (2013). *Intentional interruption: Breaking down learning barriers to transform professional practice.* Thousand Oaks, CA: Corwin Press.

Kennedy, S. Y., & Smith, J. B. (2013). The relationship between school collective reflective practice and teacher physiological efficacy sources. *Teaching and Teacher Education, 29*(1), 132–143.

Killion, J. (2015). *The feedback process: Transforming feedback for professional learning.* Oxford, OH: Learning Forward.

Konner, M. (1984). *Becoming a doctor: A journey of initiation in medical school.* New York: Penguin.

Kraft, M. A., Blazar, D., & Hogan, D. (2017). *The effect of teacher coaching on instruction and achievement: A meta-analysis of the causal evidence* (Working paper). Providence, RI: Brown University.

Kruglanski, A. W., & Webster, D. M. (1996). Motivated closing of the mind: "Seizing" and "freezing." *Psychological Bulletin, 103*(2), 263–283.

Kruse, K. (2017, July 10). *Could 'habit stacking' be the key to better results?* Accessed at www.forbes.com/sites/kevinkruse/2017/07/10/could-habit-stacking-be-the-key-to-better-results/ on August 7, 2018.

Langley, G. L., Nolan, K. M., Nolan, T. W., Norman, C. L., & Provost, L. P. (2009). *The improvement guide: A practical approach to enhancing organizational performance* (2nd ed.). San Francisco: Jossey Bass.

Leadership That Works. (2019). *7 steps for developing a coaching culture.* Accessed at www.leadershipthatworks.com/article/5037/index.cfm on October 1, 2019.

Lee, J. C., Zhang, Z., & Yin, H. (2011). A multilevel analysis of the impact of a professional learning community, faculty trust in colleagues and collective efficacy on teacher commitment to students. *Teaching and Teacher Education, 27*, 820–830.

Lee, V. E., Dedrick, R. F., & Smith, J. B. (1991). The effect of the social organization of schools on teachers' efficacy and satisfaction. *Sociology of Education, 64*(3), 190–208.

Lewin, K., & Cartwright, D. (Ed.). (1951). *Field theory in social science: Selected theoretical papers.* New York: Harper & Row.

Lipton, L., & Wellman, B. (2012). *Got data? now what? Creating and leading cultures of inquiry*. Bloomington, IN: Solution Tree Press.

Little, J. W. (1990, Summer). The persistence of privacy: autonomy and initiative in teachers' professional relations. *Teachers College Record, 91*(4), 509–536.

Lupoli, C. (2018). *Creating a culture of collaboration and coaching to improve the effectiveness of every teacher*. Accessed at http://inservice.ascd.org/creating-a-culture-of-collaboration-and-coaching-to-improve-the-effectiveness-of-every-teacher/ on July 7, 2019.

Many, T. W., Maffoni, M. J., Sparks, S. K., & Thomas, T. F. (2018). *Amplify your impact: Coaching collaborative teams in PLCs*. Bloomington, IN: Solution Tree Press.

Marzano, R. J. (2000). *Transforming classroom grading*. Alexandria VA: Association for Supervision and Curriculum Development.

Marzano, R. (2011). The art and science of teaching / making the most of instructional rounds. *Educational Leadership, 68*(5), 80–82. Accessed at www.ascd.org/publications/educational-leadership/feb11/vol68/num05/Making-the-Most-of-Instructional-Rounds.aspx on October 4, 2019.

The Merriam-Webster Dictionary. (2019). Springfield, MA: Merriam-Webster.

Mintzberg, H. (2004). *Managers not MBAs: A hard look at the soft practice of managing and management development*. London: Financial Times Prentice Hall.

Moody, M. (2017). *Creating a culture of coaching to support teachers in every school*. Accessed at https://edsource.org/2017/creating-a-culture-of-coaching-to-support-teachers-in-every-school/591856 on June 30, 2019.

Mook, M. (2017). *A lesson (from a school) in building a coaching culture*. Accessed at www.bizjournals.com/bizjournals/how-to/human-resources/2017/10/a-lesson-from-a-school-in-building-a-coaching.html on September 25, 2019.

Moolenaar, N. M., Sleegers, P. J. C., & Daly, A. J. (2012). Teaming up: Linking collaboration networks, collective efficacy, and student achievement. *Teaching and Teacher Education, 28*(2), 251–262.

Mulvey, P. W., & Klein, H. J. (1998). The impact of perceived loafing and collective efficacy on group goal processes and group performance. *Organizational Behavior and Human Decision Processes, 74*(1), 62–87.

Newmann, F. M., Rutter, R. A., & Smith, M. S. (1989). Organizational factors that affect school sense of efficacy, community, and expectations. *Sociology of Education, 62*(4), 221–238.

Nystrom, P. C., & Starbuck, W. H. (1984). To avoid organizational crises, unlearn. *Organizational Dynamics, 12*(4), 53–65.

Park, S., Hironaka, S., Carver, P., and Nordstrum, L. (2013). *Continuous improvement in education*. Stanford, CA: Carnegie Foundation for the Advancement of Teaching.

Pfeffer, J. (2007). *What were they thinking? Unconventional wisdom about management.* Boston: Harvard Business School Press.

Pfeffer, J., & Sutton, R. I. (2000). *The knowing-doing gap: How smart companies turn knowledge into action.* Boston: Harvard Business School Press.

Plattner, H. (n.d.). [Brochure from the design institute at Stanford]. Stanford, CA: Hasso Plattner Institute of Design.

Red Clay Consolidated School District. (2018). *Professional learning communities (PLC) overview and guidelines.* Wilmington, DE.

Reeves, D. B. (2004). The case against zero. *Phi Delta Kappan, 86*(4), 324–325.

Reeves, D. B. (2007/2008). Leading to change / making strategic planning work. *Educational Leadership, 65*(4), 86–87.

Reeves, D. B. (2011). *Finding your leadership focus.* New York: Teachers College Press.

Ross, J. A., & Gray, P. (2006) Transformational leadership and teacher commitment to organizational values: The mediating effects of collective teacher efficacy. *School Effectiveness and School Improvement, 17*(2), 179–199.

Rosenholtz, S. J. (1989). *Teachers' workplace: The social organization of schools.* New York: Addison-Wesley Longman.

Sagor, R. (2000). *Guiding school improvement with action research.* Alexandria, VA: Association for Supervision and Curriculum Development.

Sagor, R. (2010). *Collaborative action research for professional learning communities.* Bloomington, IN: Solution Tree Press.

Sagor, R., & Williams, C. D. V. (2017). *The action research guidebook: A process for pursuing equity and excellence in education* (3rd ed.). Thousand Oaks, CA: Corwin Press.

Senge, P. (1990). *The fifth discipline: The art and practice of the learning organization.* New York: Bantam Doubleday Dell.

Schmoker, M. (1999). *Results: The key to continuous school improvement* (2nd ed.). Alexandria, VA: Association for Supervision and Curriculum Development.

Schmoker, M. (2006). *Results now: How we can achieve unprecedented improvements in teaching and learning.* Alexandria, VA: Association for Supervision and Curriculum Development.

Sparks, S. K., & Many, T. W. (2011). A thousand conversations. *TEPSA News, 68*(3).

Supovitz, J. A., & Christman, J. B. (2003). Developing communities of instructional practice: Lessons from Cincinnati and Philadelphia. *CPRE Policy Briefs.*

Thomas, T. F. (2015, November 23). *Pathways for coaching collaborative teams.* Presented at East Detroit Public Schools, Eastpointe, MI.

Thomas, T. F. (2019). *The implications of instructional coaches' participation in professional learning community collaborative team meetings.* Unpublished manuscript.

Toussaint, S.-L. (2018, July 19). *Academic intervention support for high school: Improving student success in core content areas* (unpublished report for Mapleton School District Superintendent, Charlotte Ciancio). Denver, CO.

Tschannen-Moran, M., & Barr, M. (2004). Fostering student learning: The relationship of collective teacher efficacy and student achievement. *Leadership and Policy in Schools, 3*(3), 189–209.

Value Based Management. (2016). *Result oriented management.* Accessed at www.valuebasedmanagement.net/methods_result_oriented_management.html on August 23, 2019.

van Nieuwerburgh, C., & Passmore, J. (2012). Creating coaching cultures for learning. In C. van Nieuwerburgh (Ed.), *Coaching in education: Getting better results for students, educators and parents* (pp. 153–172). London: Karnac Pressure Books.

Visible Learning. (n.d.) *Collective teacher efficacy (CTE) according to John Hattie.* Accessed at http://visible-learning.org/2018/03/collective-teacher-efficacy-hattie on September 24, 2019.

Voelkel, R. H., Jr., & Chrispeels, J. H. (2017). Understanding the link between professional learning communities and teacher collective efficacy. *School Effectiveness and School Improvement, 28*(4), 505–526.

Whitmore, J. (2009). *Coaching for performance: Growing people, performance and purpose* (4th ed.). London: Nicholas Brealey.

INDEX

C

Q

R

S

T

U

V

W